DIALOGUE PREACHING

THE SHARED SERMON

DIALOGUE PREACHING

THE SHARED SERMON

William D. Thompson
Gordon C. Bennett

THE JUDSON PRESS • VALLEY FORGE

CONTENTS

Preface   7

1. How Dialogue Preaching Began   15

2. The Congregation in Dialogue   24

3. Dialogue in the Chancel   37

4. The Values of Dialogue Preaching   65

5. An Anthology of Dialogue Sermons   73

   Dialogue of Support: "If I Should Die"   75
        Ralph H. Lightbody and William D. Thompson

   Dialogue of Support: "The Many Masks of Christians"   86
        Theodore E. Whitacre and David Martin

   Dialogue of Support: "The Unity We Seek"   93
        Robert H. Bonthius and Paul E. Waldschmidt

   Dialogue of Inquiry: "No Further Trek"   113
        Harlan London and Robert Bolton

   Dialogue of Conflict: "Preacher Meets Hippie"   122
        D. Richard Hepler

Dialogue of Conflict: "Ins and Outs"   128
    Vern Campbell and Fred Libbey

Dialogue of Conflict: "Don't Blame God"   137
    Rev. Howard E. Friend, Jr., Robert Shortino,
    Ron Van Norstrand, Ron Fountain, Andy Borgogna,
    Richard Swartout

Composite Dialogue: "You Are the Man"   147
    Gordon C. Bennett

PREFACE

"DISCUSSION BETWEEN PRIEST AND PEOPLE will replace sermons at many Sunday masses in the Hobart [Australia] archdiocese," read the *National Catholic Reporter* of October 18, 1967. ". . . Each Sunday, in the first half of 1968, parishioners will receive printed sheets giving a condensation of the council's teaching on a particular topic. On the following Sunday, discussion of this topic by priest and people will replace the sermon." The archdiocesan senate of priests evidently concluded that the way to make people aware of the teachings of the Second Vatican Council was through preparatory dialogue rather than having them listen to a standard sermon.

A few months later, *Time* (May 17, 1968) reported that church dialogue was rapidly spreading in the United States as well:

> Today, more and more U.S. clergymen are letting the people in the pew talk back by experimenting with "dialogue sermons" as an alternate to the pulpit monologue. One reason for this communal approach to the exposition of God's word is that today's educated congregations are unwilling to put up with authoritarian preaching that lacks the stamp of credibility. Advocates of the dialogue sermon point out that since industry, government and education have discovered the virtue of the seminar and the conference, the church should also explore this avenue of intellectual discovery.[1]

More recently, on July 16, 1968, the World Council of

[1] *Time*, May 17, 1968, p. 80.

7

Churches meeting in Uppsala, Sweden, adopted a final report on "The Worship of God in a Secular Age," which includes a challenge to the pulpit ministry: "The churches have traditionally known the power of the preached word to convince men of the call of God to them in their situation. Yet, in our day, the sermon as prepared and preached by one man comes increasingly under question. In these circumstances the traditional sermon ought to be supplemented by new means of proclamation." The report goes on to mention dialogue, drama, and visual arts as forms of presentation that may help modern man understand the Christian message.

We agree with the World Council report that the traditional sermon needs to be supplemented by something new — like dialogue. The reports from Hobart, Australia, and from *Time* magazine describe one increasingly popular form of dialogue preaching, the *congregational dialogue*. There is another kind of dialogue preaching which we call *chancel dialogue* because it usually takes place within the chancel of the church. It is a conversation between two or more persons rather than an open discussion involving the whole congregation. Our intention in this book is to describe and illustrate both forms of dialogue preaching, and to provide help for persons who wish to engage in it.

Dialogue comes in many shapes and sizes. A football coach's pep talk, a glance between lovers, a shouted comment between spot welders in a machine shop, an atmosphere involving complex human relationships between races in a Kentucky village may all be dialogical. Reuel Howe's definition of dialogue grows out of Martin Buber's statement of the "I-Thou" relationship. Buber spoke of a life of dialogue based on person-to-person relationships, averring that human selfhood develops only in community with other selves. Let Dr. Howe make it unmistakably clear: "Dialogue . . . is that interaction between persons in which one of them seeks to give himself as he is to the other, and seeks also to know the other as the other is." [2]

Note very carefully the difference between dialogue as principle and dialogue as method. If dialogue is understood as an approach to people, a lecture may be dialogical, even though

[2] Reuel Howe, *The Miracle of Dialogue* (New York: The Seabury Press, Inc., 1963), p. 37.

only one person is talking, *provided* the lecturer takes into account the experiences which are brought by all the people to the whole speaking-listening encounter. Conversely, a platform dialogue in which the speakers fail to relate to each other or to their audience may have a monological effect, even though two persons are talking.

There is no doubt about it: communicative preaching is dialogical and always has been. It is characterized by the preacher's concern for the attitudes, experiences, and needs of his people. In every aspect of his ministry he must listen to them and respond appropriately to their needs and feelings. In this book, however, we are not dealing primarily with dialogue as a principle, but with dialogue as a method of preaching. *We define dialogue preaching to be an act within the context of public worship in which two or more persons engage in a verbal exchange as the sermon or message.* Both congregational dialogue and chancel dialogue fall within this definition.

Keep in mind that we are talking about dialogue within the experience of public worship—the period when Christians gather in the Protestant "morning service" or the Roman Catholic mass or the Anglican "morning prayer and sermon." Many clergy use dialogue as an adjunct to worship. For example, some pastors seek feedback from laymen in sermon discussion groups which gather outside the sanctuary. Increasingly, pastors are bringing people together during the week prior to the sermon to study the Scripture text and help construct the sermon.[3] The dialogue method is in wide use in the religious education program of nearly every church body — in church schools, home study groups, retreats, and other settings. Dialogue is one of the most popular techniques of religious broadcasters, on both radio and television. The concern of this book is solely the dialogue which takes place in public worship, though every effort to utilize dialogue as a technique for enriching the growth and witness of the church is applauded.

[3] For further information on sermon preparation groups, see:

Reuel Howe, *Partners in Preaching* (New York: The Seabury Press, Inc., 1967).

Clyde Reid, *The Empty Pulpit* (New York: Harper & Row, Publishers, Inc., 1967).

William D. Thompson, *A Listener's Guide to Preaching* (Nashville: Abingdon Press, 1966).

Has the traditional monological sermon had its day? We think not. It has stood the test of time, in spite of what its detractors say, and is still one of the church's basic tools for communicating its faith. Dialogue preaching is not proposed as a substitute for monologue preaching, but rather as a supplement to it. We do not advocate that the pastor share his pulpit every Sunday, or substitute for pews a roomful of chairs which can be pulled into circles to form "buzz groups." Undoubtedly, new churches will be constructed to allow for such groupings. We do suggest that dialogue belongs as surely in the church's public worship as in its classrooms, and that the pastor use it as often as he finds it meaningful for himself and his people. For those who are bold enough to experiment, there are still many ways to proclaim God's truth. The results of experimenting with dialogue preaching may be surprisingly refreshing.

What justification is there for the growing use of dialogue preaching? One could certainly build a rationale for it within the field of learning theory: a great deal of research points to the personality changes which frequently result from meaningful dialogue. Another case for dialogue preaching could be constructed from the field of group dynamics, which documents the values of personal interaction in the group process. Similarly, modern communication theory, with its source-receiver orientation and its stress on communication as a dynamic process involving constant feedback, adds support for the use of dialogue in the pulpit. It is quite valid to speak of identification, catharsis, involvement, and other psychological concepts to support and describe the use of dialogue preaching. Our purpose, however, is not to set forth an exhaustive psychology of dialogue preaching. Perhaps the description of what is being done and the effects will be its own justification and will pave the way for a more complete psychological analysis in the future.

We do wish to comment on two schools of thought which are profoundly affecting the theory and practice of religious communication: drama and Marshall McLuhan. We cannot determine whether there is more interest in chancel drama now than there used to be, but apparently there is a new awareness of the relationship between pulpit and theatre. Ronald Sleeth speaks of the gospel as the "Great Dramatic Event" and argues that the preacher's task is to reveal it in a persuasive fashion.

The basic principle of dramatization is to place truth in such imaginative form that people respond through several of their senses. For the preacher, it means presenting the Gospel in such a way that people respond to it with their whole being—they virtually participate in the Gospel itself. When a preacher presents the Gospel in dramatic form he and the congregation participate together; the sermon becomes a shared experience in which all are vital participants in the drama unfolding before their eyes.[4]

The question is frequently asked, "When does preaching become drama?" We have no final answer to this. Drama has been defined as a representation of reality. Monological preaching is certainly a commentary on reality and may indeed be an interpretation of reality as it intersects the gospel, but it is generally not a representation of reality. Dialogue preaching, however, may approximate drama. If the preacher is holding a conversation with a hippie about love, and if the person who takes the part of the hippie dresses in appropriate garb and assumes the role of a hippie from start to finish, we have both authentic drama and, quite possibly, effective preaching.

One of the strengths of dialogue preaching is its affinity with drama, which provides the opportunity to use dramatic elements such as real conflict. The line between some kinds of preaching and drama is thin indeed, if there is really a line to be drawn. To argue disdainfully that dialogue preaching is just "play-acting," as some do, is to permit a fixed conception of preaching to close one's mind to the fact that God may use many ways to get his Word across to people. We suspect that the best preaching is drama and the best drama is preaching. Dialogue tends to put God's truth visually "on stage" where the congregation may identify with it, or at least join in a common search for Christian meaning with the minister.

Marshall McLuhan's dictum that *the medium is the message* also has a direct bearing on our discussion.[5] Dialogue as a medium for the proclamation of the gospel is a reflection of the fact that the gospel is living dialogue. It is the nature of God to seek man and the nature of man to seek God; they have always attempted to relate meaningfully to each other. Christianity also

[4] Ronald Sleeth, *Persuasive Preaching* (New York: Harper & Row, Publishers, Inc., 1956), pp. 66-67.

[5] Marshall McLuhan, *Understanding Media: The Extensions of Man* (New York: McGraw-Hill Book Company, 1964).

posits a second dialogue: that between man and his fellow man, which is also a religious experience, since man is created in the image of God. The vertical and horizontal beams of the cross represent these two essential dialogues which are a part of both the Christian's essence and his daily walk. So it may be argued that dialogue is a technique of worship which more accurately represents the nature of Christian experience than does the monologue sermon. The medium of dialogue preaching is the message that God and man are in some kind of dialogue because of their natures. If the substance of the dialogue sermon is faithful to the gospel, it will articulate *and demonstrate* the possibility of the dialogue becoming an experience that is mutually acceptable and affirmative.

The authors have engaged in dialogue preaching often enough themselves to recommend it heartily to others. This study is not only the result of their personal experience with it; it is also an investigation of the technique as it is practiced by others. William Thompson has compiled an extensive file of dialogue sermons which he has analyzed and discussed with graduate seminary students. Gordon Bennett prepared a master's thesis on dialogue preaching based on questionnaires which were returned by a large number of pastors in many denominations and locations.[6]

Of this we are certain: the dialogue sermon is being increasingly employed by creative pastors who are keenly concerned about reaching the people who sit in the pews. Of the 151 alumni of the Institute for Advanced Pastoral Study in Bloomfield Hills, Michigan, who responded to the questionnaire, 59.6 percent said that they had used this form of communication; many others were planning to use it. Nearly all who had tried it were enthusiastic about their experience.

In the first chapter of this book we attempt to jump from lily pad to lily pad without getting wet. We define dialogue in somewhat greater detail and sketch out a brief history of dialogue as a means of communication. The rest of the book describes and illustrates the basic types of congregational and chancel dialogue, and deals with some of the objections raised to its use. The an-

---

[6] Gordon C. Bennett, *Dialogue Preaching: A Descriptive Study of an Emerging Technique.* Unpublished Master's thesis, Temple University, Philadelphia, Pa., 1967.

thology of chancel dialogues should serve to give some flavor of what this kind of dialogue sounds like and to stimulate readers who wish to use this method.

This is a pioneer study; it will provoke many questions which cannot now be answered. We hope that the reader will understand that we are exploring a fairly new technique which has not been thoroughly tested or evaluated. Our analysis may not be as sophisticated as those which will follow when there is more to analyze. We hope, at least, to expose dialogue preaching to some who will find the method and the results as exciting as we have.

Dialogue preaching undoubtedly startles some and shocks others. It is anathema to the unbending traditionalist. We feel that it is God's gift to his church for a critical period in her life.

And why shouldn't it be? After all, it was Jesus who spoke of the fierce necessity of putting new wine into new wineskins.

W. D. T.
G. C. B.

1

HOW DIALOGUE
PREACHING BEGAN

DIALOGUE IS AN ANCIENT FORM of human expression. Virtually no human communication takes place without dialogue; it is essential to any kind of meaningful interaction between persons or groups. No education takes place without dialogue. If man cannot be human alone, then dialogue is that basic ingredient which gives man his meaning in the context of his relationships. Let us sketch some of the high points in the development of dialogue as a spoken exchange between two or more persons.

Beginning with the Greeks, we can illustrate the use of the dialogue form for various purposes. Plato is notable among classical scholars and rhetoricians who found it useful as a teaching device, and his Socratic dialogues provide antecedents for the question-answer technique used in the classroom, forum, and pulpit today. Dialogues are part of several extant manuscripts by Cicero and others dating immediately before and after Christ. The growth of the law court as an institution and the teaching of forensics prompted the development of an additional specialized form of dialogue in ancient Greece and Rome — the debate. While this formal pro-and-con discussion of issues did not always take the guise of a Socratic quest for truth, it was an attempt to explore and interpret truth orally, through the process of conflict and resolution. Biblical materials also contain much dialogue, though it is usually reported as conversation between individuals or as discussion between man and God.

From early times dialogue was seen as both a purpose and a

form of worship. Biblical personalities would agree with a modern commentator that "What happens in worship ... is that God speaks personally to us and that we speak to Him in reply."[1] Dialogue as a form in worship was an early part of Hebrew ritual, especially in some of the psalms which apparently were spoken, chanted, or sung antiphonally in temple or synagogue worship. These hymns of the Hebrews often developed into liturgies in which there was an interchange between speakers or singers which one investigator has grouped under four headings: liturgies of entrance, liturgies of praise and thanksgiving, prophetic liturgies, and liturgies of supplication.[2] For example, we can understand Psalm 136, containing the repeated response "for his steadfast love endures for ever,"[3] as a liturgy of national thanksgiving which was a dialogue between priest and congregation. Leslie sees Psalm 24 as a liturgy of entrance in which the pilgrims stood before the gates of the temple and sang the question, "Who shall ascend the hill of the Lord? And who shall stand in his holy place?" And the priestly choir within the gates would respond, "He who has clean hands and a pure heart, who does not lift up his soul to what is false, and does not swear deceitfully."[4] Soon the pilgrims entered the temple and the liturgy continued in its hymn of praise to God.

Jesus often taught in answer to questions posed by skeptics, by his disciples, or by himself. A British advocate of dialogue preaching writes:

> The Gospels are full of dialogue, not long and brilliant homilies. The genuine evangelist is not so much the solitary master of words as the engaged servant of the Word—the Word which speaks *to* as well as *through* the preacher.
>
> "As the Father hath sent me, so send I you." Hence, to mark Jesus at noonday with the woman at the well of Sychar, at midnight with Nicodemus in the city, at evening with the travellers on the Emmaus road, as dawn breaks with the fishermen at the lakeside—is to hear the Divine dialogue which is, at once, the faithful preacher's pattern and his enduring inspiration.[5]

[1] Wilhelm Hahn, *Worship and Congregations*, Geoffrey Buswell, trans. (Richmond: John Knox Press, 1963), p. 16.

[2] Elmer Leslie, *The Psalms* (Nashville: Abingdon Press, 1949).

[3] Psalm 136:1.

[4] Psalm 24:3, 4.

[5] Brian A. Greet, "Dialogue Preaching," *The Expository Times* (Scotland), Vol. LXXVIII, February, 1967, p. 150.

The worship of the early Christian church, like its evangelism, was personal and informal. There was little structure and elaborate liturgy developed slowly. The New Testament reports conversation between the disciples of Jesus and the people they confronted in their attempts to spread the "good news," but there is little clear statement in the New Testament of the kind of worship used by the first-century Christians. We do have St. Paul's interpretation of worship in 1 Corinthians 14:26-40, which implies that there was no sermon as we know it today, but that members of the congregation were free to share orally, as they were moved by the Spirit, their concerns and their ideas. "Each person in the assembly was free to contribute his own thoughts regarding the interpretation and understanding of God's Word," [6] writes a Roman Catholic scholar who uses this evidence as part of his rationale for the dialogue homily as it is employed in the Catholic church today.

There were no professional clergy in the early Christian church. Later, when the sermon became a formal discourse by an ordained minister, pastor, or priest, there was still a good deal of congregational response, some of it spontaneous. Chrysostom usually began preaching with the words: "Blessed be God. Peace be unto you," followed by a congregational response wishing God's blessing on him. The renowned Augustine of Hippo, who preached about 400 A.D., seemed to be engaged in almost constant dialogue with his auditors, who would respond with applause and comments during the reading of the text and the homily.

> St. Augustine was known to ask questions of the people present if he wanted to impress upon them the importance of what he was saying (cf. Sermon 101, 9); and in his *De Doctrina Christiana* (4, 39), he explicitly advocates this practice. Augustine also made his listeners repeat passages after him. While preaching a sermon at Carthage, for example, he said: "Now all say after me: 'Charity from a pure heart.' (I Tim. 1:5)"; then all his listeners repeated this phrase after him. Often the people would voice their approval—or disapproval—of what Augustine said by shouting acclamations or beating their breasts, for example, when Augustine spoke of the need for contrition.[7]

As worship developed more structure and was formalized by

[6] Richard Leliaert, "The Dialogue Homily: Theory," *Preaching*, Vol. 2, No. 1, January-February 1967, p. 20.

[7] *Ibid.*, p. 21.

the medieval church, this kind of congregational spontaneity virtually disappeared. Christian liturgy, however, has included many kinds of congregational responses to the present day. Early in the development of worship, the congregation answered "Amen" at the close of a prayer, which made of prayer a corporate event. Today, choral and congregational responses are spoken or sung by worshipers in many communions, and even the less liturgical Protestant congregations sing the Gloria and the Doxology, as well as participating in the responsive readings. While the Roman Catholic church historically has shown less concern for lay leadership and participation in worship, the recent liberalization of its liturgy, the increasing use of lay leaders, and the "dialogue" or "community" mass authorized by Pope Pius XI has begun to reverse Catholic policy and practices in worship.[8]

Formal dialogue, in the sense of a planned, structured exchange between two or more persons, was not generally employed in the Christian church until medieval times. Then dialogue was adopted for evangelistic and didactic uses by the church. It became a popular form of teaching. One could set up a "straw man" and knock him down, making it appear that the arguments in defense of the faith were superior to those of the opponent or skeptic. This approach is described humorously by two pastors, Alan J. Pickering and Hudson B. Phillips, in their introduction to a dialogue sermon delivered to students of the University of Nebraska:

> The speaker for the negative side was considered to be a representation of the Powers of darkness and anti-Christ—even Satan himself. For that reason the speaker for the negative side was called the "Advocatus Diaboli", or the "Advocate of the Devil." The speaker for the affirmative side, on the other hand, was called the "Vindicatus Deii", or the "Vindicator of God." Because of my personality traits, I will take the latter role; while Mr. Pickering, for quite obvious reasons, will be perfectly type-cast as the Advocate of the Devil.

Barrett and Casserley elaborate on medieval practice:

> A somewhat similar technique was employed by the Catholic Church of the Middle Ages—still is employed by the Roman Church—in the proceedings which lead to the canonization of saints. Those who argue in favor

[8] George Hedley, *Christian Worship* (New York: The Macmillan Company, 1953), p. 190.

of the canonization of the saints are opposed by a devil's advocate, *advocatus diaboli*, whose task it is to state all the arguments against canonization. At a later date, some of the Jesuit preachers used a similar technique in church and during missions. One priest proclaimed the gospel or taught the faith while another represented the point of view of the atheist or unbeliever. The central idea was to exhibit to the people the power and capacity of Christian thought to meet and overcome difficulties and objections.[9]

In the medieval period, formal dialogue generally had didactic purposes. It was used to indoctrinate the people with the dogma of the church. Many forms of the question-answer approach became standard manuals of instruction, or catechisms, a device still employed by many communions as a method of instruction. Originally the catechism was used prior to baptism or within the baptismal service itself to provide a means of judging the candidate's readiness for baptism. With the increasing use of infant baptism by the church, the catechism became a means of instruction and confirmation of the individual's membership in the church after baptism. Early questions and answers for instruction of youth centered upon the Creed, the Lord's Prayer, and the Ten Commandments, but in time many additions were made to these manuals.[10] The value of the catechism as a learning device was quite clear.

As Christianity progressed during the succeeding centuries, missionaries became involved in dialogue with the national adherents of other religions. In America, the expansion of the frontier lent itself to a kind of rebuttal preaching in which the defenders of the gospel tried to counter the obvious skepticism and immorality of the times. The so-called "Great Awakenings" in the 18th and 19th centuries were the attempt of frontier evangelists to bring Americans back to a simple and heartfelt belief in Jesus Christ as Savior and Lord. Many people on the frontiers had forgotten the God of their forefathers; their preoccupation with hewing civilization out of a wilderness tended to eclipse spiritual, non-temporal concerns.

In the early 1800's, the emotional frenzy occasioned by the camp meetings, which lacked formal structure and dignity, gave

[9] George W. Barrett and J. V. Langmead Casserley, *Dialogue on Destiny* (New York: The Seabury Press, Inc., 1955), pp. 10-11.

[10] "Catechisms," *Encyclopaedia of Religion and Ethics*, James Hastings, ed. (New York: Charles Scribner's Sons, 1951), III, pp. 251-256.

worship a circus atmosphere. People were moved by eloquent evangelists to cry out, weep, gnash their teeth, or roll on the ground as the Spirit moved them to seek the Lord. The outdoor revival services were periods of great excitement, and the common feeling was that conversion had to be accomplished through emotional upheaval. Feeling as they did that tears of penitence and shouts of glory were essential, "the Cartwrights and Finleys and hundreds of their fellows carried the throat-tightening, pulse-fluttering stimulation of frontier religion to every lonely cabin in the West." [11] Johnson Hooper in the 1840's caricatured the struggles of a preacher with a reluctant convert at an Alabama camp meeting:

> Then he tried to argy wi' me—but bless the Lord!—he couldn't do that nother! Ha! Lord! I tuk him fust in the Old Testament—bless the Lord!— and I argyed him all thro' Kings—then I throwed him into Proverbs—and from that, here we had it up and down, kleer down to the New Testament, and then I begun to see it work him! Then we got into Matthy, and from Matthy right straight along to Acts; and *thar* I throwed him! . . . Yes L-o-r-d! and h-e-r-e he is! [12]

Another example of frontier dialogue is afforded by the legendary account of Abraham Lincoln's encounter with the Methodist circuit preacher, Peter Cartwright, who at that time was Lincoln's opponent for Congress. Lincoln wandered into one of Cartwright's revival services and Cartwright spotted him. "All those who want to go to heaven, please stand up," said Cartwright, and all stood up except Lincoln. "Will all those who do not want to go to hell stand up?" intoned Cartwright. All stood except Lincoln. Then said Cartwright in his gravest voice, "I observe that all of you save one indicated that you did not desire to go to hell. All of you save one expressed the wish to go to heaven. The sole exception is Mr. Lincoln, who did not respond to either invitation. May I inquire of you, Mr. Lincoln, where you are going?"

Abe Lincoln rose slowly, and slowly did he speak: "I came here as a respectful listener. I did not know that I was to be singled

---

[11] Bernard A. Weisberger, *They Gathered at the River* (Boston: Little, Brown, and Company, 1958), p. 48. Copyright © by Bernard A. Weisberger. By permission of Little, Brown, and Company.

[12] *Ibid.*, p. 49, quoting Johnson Hooper, *Simon Suggs' Adventures* (New York, 1928), pp. 83-93.

out by Brother Cartwright. I believe in treating religious matters with due solemnity. I admit that the questions propounded by Brother Cartwright are of great importance. I did not feel called upon to answer as the rest did. Brother Cartwright asks me directly where I am going. I desire to reply with equal directness: I am going to Congress!" That response of Lincoln's broke up the meeting and serves as a warning to aspiring dialogue preach- ers: be prepared for the consequences!

The spontaneous informality of frontier worship has come to us in various forms today, especially in some of our smaller sects and non-liturgical churches where the "Amen" and "You tell 'em, preacher!" still ring out during the sermon. There is a sense of spiritual excitement and a feeling of divine movement among the participants in many of these services where vocal freedom is permitted and acceptable for the worshiper as well as the leader of worship. The preacher has the advantage of hearing reactions, a kind of immediate verbal feedback, during his sermonic presentation. Most of our main-line Protestant churches, however, have drifted far from this experience into a more stately, dignified, sometimes antiseptic worship where any overt response during the sermon is literally frowned upon!

We have seen dialogue develop within worship and become formalized in the liturgy of the church. We have considered its development as a teaching device which was generally used apart from worship in the catechism class, but was also employed within worship on occasion. We have suggested that dialogue was one form of the attempt to evangelize from earliest times, although it was usually on an informal, conversational level. Formal pulpit dialogue, essentially a recent development, may be an outgrowth of the historic Christian concern for the unchurched, and an attempt to come to grips with their thinking. This concern persists in the confrontation between church and world that has prompted much of the dialogue preaching that is taking place today. Note, for example, the work of the Rev. Hugh Suassey, Jr., and the Rev. Joseph McCulloch.

Mr. Suassey teams with a member of his congregation who is a practicing psychiatrist, and together they preach once a month in their New York parish, conversing together on the chancel platform. The Rev. Joseph McCulloch has for three years been drawing standing-room-only crowds into the Anglican church of

St. Mary-le-bow in London to hear his dialogues with illustrious visitors from various walks of life — writers, broadcasters, stage personalities, musicians, politicians, architects — many of whom are not in sympathy with the church. A good measure of the success of this experiment, according to Mr. McCulloch, lies in the openings for counseling which arise after the dialogues, and in continuing conversations. "When the dialogue has been particularly lively, knots of people are to be seen afterwards in Cheapside, continuing the discussion on the way back to work. This is all to the good. The worst thing that can happen to the church in 'no-churchman's land' is to be politely suffered and ignored." [13] Mr. McCulloch feels that he has found a way to bridge the gap between religion and culture:

> In such an experimental field one was bound to progress only by trial and error. Our first series of dialogues was moderately successful in attracting a fairly large audience each week, mainly because of the novelty of the idea and its *mise en scene*. But I had cautiously invited only fellow-churchmen to occupy the other pulpit, and our discourse, however widely we ranged on matters of topical interest, was still the Cabots talking to the Lowells. At least that was some advance on talking only to God, but towards a breakthrough between Church and non-Church it did not go very far . . . It is when the Church is in dialogue with the world on equal terms that the truth of Christianity is seen to be a live issue and to touch the common life deeply at every point. . . .
>
> Many people in "non-church land" are in the process of weighing things up, and trying to make up their minds about human existence and what may lie behind it. They do not know what to believe. They are by no means anti-Christian, but have many misgivings about the Church, as indeed about most institutions claiming authority over them from the past. They have long since given up listening to us with any real attention because they have heard us, as they think, *ad nauseam*. But what if we could show ourselves capable to listen to them, of being genuinely concerned. . . . They might then begin to give us a second hearing, and when we spoke, to feel that we were no longer speaking from outside their situation.[14]

The dialogic method today is seldom such a bald encounter between the church and the world, but a variety of dialogic styles and techniques are being employed. In Detroit, for example, a Protestant minister who is an amateur ventriloquist has engaged a dummy in conversation during the worship service in

[13] Joseph McCulloch, "Dialogue with the World," *New Christian* (England), November 3, 1966, p. 8.

[14] *Ibid.*

his working-class church. The co-ministers at the First Methodist Church of Germantown, Philadelphia, Pa., make it a point to have occasional dialogues "in which . . . issues are batted back and forth between pulpit and lectern to the delight of the congregation. . . ." [15] A college-town minister, the Rev. John D. Banks, has written and presented a series of platform-trialogues on the seven deadly sins, including the views of "Mr. Natural Man," "Mr. Straight and-Narrow," and "Mr. Christian." Another pastor had a Negro gentleman rise suddenly from the congregation to quarrel with some of his statements about civil rights. Another engaged in a dialogue sermon with the church organ — presumably with some help from the organist!

Other preachers are using clergy-clergy dialogues, clergy-lay dialogues, and clergy-youth dialogues on a variety of topics. Some clergy are seizing the opportunity for ecumenical contact to invite representatives of other faiths to share the pulpit with them, developing dialogues between Catholic and Protestant clergy, and between Christian ministers and Jewish rabbis. Some pastors are calling it a dialogue when they preach a brief message, and then invite questions and discussion from the congregation. This form is becoming more frequent in Catholic parishes where it is called the "dialogue homily." What is called dialogue, then, comes in a startling variety of packages.

An interest in these unusual homiletical techniques has apparently spread among both Catholic and Protestant clergy. The dialogue itself is not new: we have seen its origins reach far back into history. The present interest in this form, however, cannot be completely accounted for in terms of the continuity of use. Other influences have probably whetted interest in such pulpit innovations: the current theological emphasis on a valid encounter with the world, a search for new means of reaching the secular generation with the gospel, experimentation with new liturgical forms, the opportunity for ecumenical relationship, and also the contributions of group dynamics, psychology, and communication theory alluded to in the preface. All of these may have an impact on the current generation of preachers who seek new forms of expression — new wineskins to hold the ever-fresh new wine of the Christian gospel.

[15] M. E. Clark, W. L. Malcomson, and W. L. Molton, eds., *The Church Creative* (Nashville: Abingdon Press, 1967), p. 19.

2

THE CONGREGATION
IN DIALOGUE

"TODAY IS DIALOGUE SUNDAY," read the morning bulletin at Community Presbyterian Church in Clarendon Hills, Illinois, at which the Rev. John David Burton is pastor. The bulletin continued,

> "Dialogue" means that the last ten or fifteen minutes of the worship hour will be left for discussion on the part of the congregation. This is our third Sunday to experiment with this particular way of learning, and we encourage your participation. At the close of the sermon, the minister will simply walk out of the pulpit and stand on the Chancel floor. Members of the congregation, as they wish, may ask questions, offer suggestions or in any other way respond concerning the life of the Church in our parish and in our world. The subjects need not be limited to the sermon of the morning, and the questions and answers need not be limited to exchange between the minister and the people. After the conversation gets under way, there may be exchange of ideas from person to person in the congregation with the minister serving as moderator.

Congregational dialogue is a means of involving the congregation in worship by inviting their spontaneous questions and comments after the topic is presented. It is a kind of "talkback" or "feedback" that takes place within worship rather than after the service is over, and it promotes discussion while the ideas are still hot and fresh and debatable. Dialogue helps to eliminate typical overcommunication in which the auditors have no chance to voice the preacher's concepts immediately in order to have them restated or clarified. Apparently some Protestant pastors are using the discussion dialogue to overcome this problem, and by so doing they are overcoming the spectator mentality that has been a part of traditional worship forms. In answering a questionnaire, the Rev. John Van Zanten, who spent twenty-five years as a Presbyterian pastor, describes the merits of dialogue preaching of this type, from his own experience:

> I ought to explain that I used this technique for four years in a small city church in the Bronx, New York. We would have a twenty minute worship period and then I would take off my gown and come down in the front of the sanctuary, between the pews, and make a presentation for about twenty-five minutes, usually on a Biblical subject. . . . Then the people would make comments and ask questions. Often these would go far afield from the subject. I found it to be alive and exciting.

Pastors using this method generally find it "alive and exciting," but most of them do not make the initial presentation as long as twenty-five minutes. Ten or fifteen minutes is the general average, which leaves a more adequate time for discussion if the total service of worship is to last one hour. Among those who are employing this technique, some of the most enthusiastic are Roman Catholic clergymen. In fact, what Catholics call the dialogue homily seems to be almost exclusively this kind of congregational dialogue. A Catholic graduate student describes it like this:

> The dialogue homily is that type of homily in which the people discuss the significance of the day's liturgy instead of hearing a formal sermon by the priest. It functions so as to make the people active, forcing them to penetrate and apply the Scriptures for themselves. In this way the Scriptures become more relevant to the people, since they talk about them in terms of the problems which they encounter and not in those of the priests.[1]

The Rev. Gerard Cleator, the author of this statement, is probably a pioneer in doing significant research on the dialogue homily. He analyzed the external structure of the dialogue homily in nine different cases of Roman Catholic worship as part of a report submitted at the University of Wisconsin in 1966. Father Cleator administered questionnaires to worshipers in which he attempted to discover their attitudes toward this type of presentation and their opinions about its value. Thirty-one of fifty respondents gave unqualified answers to the effect that the dia-

---

[1] Rev. Gerard Cleator, O. P., "Experiments in the Dialogue Homily," *Preaching*, Vol. III, No. 5, p. 22.

logue homily was more meaningful than their usual mass. We must keep in mind, however, that (1) Father Cleator's respondents were probably young people, for the most part, and (2) as the author admits, Catholic preaching in the Wisconsin area has traditionally been weak, so that some of the worshipers might have regarded anything different as an improvement! But discounting such factors, we must agree that Father Cleator's findings give a resounding vote of approval to this form of worship.

Father Cleator found that the priests who led the worship experience did not dominate discussion, moralize during it, or summarize it at the close. They simply opened with a brief exposition or a statement of purpose, played policeman when necessary to guide the ensuing discussion, then brought it to a close when it seemed appropriate. Worshipers who filled out his questionnaires listed these values of the dialogue homily, in order of frequency: (1) the people are more active in the dialogue homily than during the traditional mass (the word "involvement" was stressed), (2) there was a greater variety of ideas expressed than normally, (3) the homily was more relevant to current problems and individual needs, (4) the example of their peers (in speaking out) encouraged them spiritually, and (5) the homily built up a community feeling in the congregation.

Experiential worship is the title given to another form of congregational dialogue by the Western Behavioral Sciences Institute in La Jolla, California. Led by project director W. H. McGaw, Jr., congregations of more than one thousand people have participated in small-group discussion sermons which generally involved not more than six persons per group. The approach blends psychology, communications theory, theology, and drama, with a heavy dose of group sensitivity training.

Typically, the only monologue was Scripture reading and a brief sermon, followed by a variety of personal and group experiences designed to involve the worshipers in experiencing at the deepest level the insights of the sermon. They were asked to close their eyes to employ fantasy in which, for example, their two selves could debate the implications of adopting an attitude of unconditional love for their family life. They were then asked to share their fantasy with the group. To experience the reality of trusting, the group formed a tight circle, standing around one member who went limp and allowed himself to be passed from person to person. Subgroups of two — dyads — faced each other in the attempt to "know" each other at greater depth: they closed their eyes and explored with their hands the contours of each other's face. These same dyads could also look into each other's eyes and tell "what I like most about you." In one service, parishioners moved into the main aisle, joining hands to form a living chain representing "the vine" while other groups linked arms in their places and joined with worshipers in the aisles to form "the branches" of the living church.

While tradition-oriented persons may object to these procedures, project leaders have been amazed at the low level of resistance in most parishes. One conservative Roman Catholic parish reports that 80 to 85 percent of the parishioners responded enthusiastically to this new concept of worship, and that attendance increased 25 to 30 percent after the experiential worship began. Though such a radical approach raises many questions, the early experimentation suggests that it may effect profound changes in churches of widely divergent theological and liturgical traditions, and that it is effective across such boundaries as sex, age, and race.

In a society characterized by alienation, emotional sterility, isolation, and insulation, these groups appear to hold great potential for the majority of persons whose yearning for a touch of human compassion lies just below the surface. However, the experiential worship of the type described at La Jolla puts a strong emphasis on nonverbal as well as verbal forms of communication. It has great potential for worship and has some relevance to congregational forms of dialogue. Group sensitivity techniques and related experimental worship do suggest some of the reasons why congregational dialogue is being used, and why it ought to be used.

Our rationale for congregational dialogue must focus on the corporate nature of the church, the importance of individual response to the gospel, the values of sharing, the significance of interpersonal communion, and the personalization of worship. There is a theological as well as a practical framework. Theologically speaking, many proponents argue that congregational dialogue is a tangible expression of the New Testament concept of the church as people, not institution, and of worship as an occasion for participation, not entertainment. Many feel that the

corporate nature of the church requires a common involvement
in all aspects of worship, even to the act of proclamation which
has traditionally been reserved for the clergy. We could probably
trace this argument back to the Protestant emphasis on the priesthood of all believers as it was rediscovered during the Reformation. But it is not only the Protestant clergymen who speak for
this concept today. In the November, 1966, *Newsletter of the
Catholic Homiletic Society,* a Roman Catholic author counters
the argument that the priest alone is given the mission to preach:

> Proponents of the dialogue homily point out that the Spirit can speak
> through the laymen as well as through the priest; the authority of the
> Church to teach is safeguarded by the priest whose function is that of
> "judging the spirits" rather than that of doing all the talking himself.[2]

So the congregational dialogue sermon makes visible (and
audible) the corporate structure of the community of faith, and
it makes it possible for each worshiper to express his own faith
vocally. He actually becomes part of the proclamation of the
church. He has the opportunity to state convictions which he
may have been afraid to voice previously, or he may raise questions and have ideas clarified which had been vague or hazy.
There is an exchange of ideas between pastor and people or from
person to person within the congregation which may be very
profitable, provided that the experience is more than a mutual
sharing of ignorance. If the mood of worship has captured the
spirit of reverence, sincerity, honesty, and truth, and if these
elements become integral to the discussion, it will become an
elated, exalted experience in which the worshiper finds himself
much closer to his brother and to his God. Such values are suggested in this letter from the Rev. Barry L. Ralph, pastor of the
Prince of Peace Lutheran Church, Addison, Illinois:

> We have a weekly dialogue sermon at our 8:00 A.M. service. Such a
> dialogue has been carried on weekly for well over two years . . . At our
> service, the Pastor or Vicar presents a brief introduction/exegesis on the
> text. This usually involves some textual/historical criticism and the views
> of several commentators as to interpretation. No lesson or moral is drawn
> from the text. Following the brief (no longer than two or three minutes)
> introduction, the parishioners comment on the passage, relating it to
> their lives and sharing experiences that might apply. Occasionally they ask
> questions with regard to textual meaning. The result is a live and active

[2] *Newsletter of the Catholic Homiletic Society,* November, 1966.

dialogue, without structure from the leaders, in which the congregation literally "writes" its own sermon. Such a dialogue is used as the basis for the "formal" sermon at the 9:00 and 11:30 services the following week. The preacher is thus assured of preaching to his congregation's concerns rather than his own. We believe the best preparation is prayer, not a manuscript.

An obvious value of this sharing process is that the preacher learns what his people's concerns and needs are, provided that they are open and honest in their reactions. This would avoid the problem expressed by one layman who complained that his preacher "is always scratching us where we don't itch!" Through congregational dialogue, the minister not only can hear and feel what is in the minds and hearts of his people but he can incorporate these insights within subsequent messages and within his total pastoral approach. Although it is possible for him to explore his parishioners' feelings and needs and convictions in Bible classes and other settings, the Sunday worship service offers an opportunity to reach and hear from a larger number of people than at any other time. For the very busy pastor in a multiple-staff church where his primary function is preaching, dialogue within worship may be the only way he can discover what his people are really thinking and how they feel on certain issues. Also, we have here the possibility for a vital give-and-take between the pastor and members of various other vocations. The minister who is open can learn how the bricklayer, lawyer, or trash collector faces life, what his primary problems are, and how the Christian tenets look from "out there." Dialogue preaching can be a great learning experience for a sensitive preacher.

Not only does this method serve the pastor, but it can be very beneficial to the worshiper. For one thing, he is made aware of the importance of a personal response to the gospel. He begins to understand that Christianity is more than sitting in a pew on Sunday morning and absorbing from the pulpit a predigested diet of doctrine and ethics. He now finds that he must share, he must respond, he must articulate his faith, and in the process he can make it his own. He learns that his witness is a significant part in the total witness of the church, and he who stands up to speak before the entire congregation on Sunday morning now finds it much easier to speak the word of faith to Harry or Joe at the office on Monday.

Certainly a practical effect of such an experience is that the

layman finds that worship is relevant to life, after all, and even to
his own experience. He hears the great tenets of the faith restated
by his neighbors in the terms of their experience; he concentrates
on the discussion in which he is a part because he finds that it is
an application of doctrine to life. Consequently, through this
involvement he is more able to retain what he hears and he may
even internalize it and act upon it. As the Rev. John Van Zanten
puts it,

> . . . the advantage is that the people feel they can participate intellectually
> and vocally in the process. They find it challenging and interesting. The
> pastor finds the service much more alive for him. People remember and
> are affected by what they participate in.

In addition, the dialogue process may give some unity to a
congregation that is large and geographically scattered. If the
worship leader requires people to give their names as they make
comments, members of a large church may become acquainted
for the first time. This will help overcome the problem of bigness
and the impersonal nature of many congregations where an individual may enter the sanctuary, sit silently for an hour and
then leave, not having communicated with a single human
being except perhaps for the minister whose hand is grimly
wrung in the foyer when the worshiper makes his exit. If this is
the only time the person goes to church during the week, the
kind of involvement we have described may be his only opportunity to become a spiritual and audible part of that congregation.

Enough for the rationale. Assuming that the reader is bursting
to try this method, just how does he go about it? He must realize,
first, that this technique cannot be sprung on an unsuspecting
congregation without some sort of warning. Especially in a parish where innovations in worship have been seldom attempted,
the minister or priest must somehow prepare his congregation for
the experiment. One way to do this is by utilizing the dialogue
format in smaller meetings such as a midweek prayer service, or
an adult study group. The pastor can also educate his congregation about the nature of the church and the function of preaching from his pulpit, through his parish paper, or in small groups.
He may want to lead a study of worship with his board of dea-
cons, elders, lay advisory board, or whoever is responsible for the
worship program in the local parish. In many ways he may let

his people know that something new is coming and he can prepare them to await it expectantly and enter into it with joy and
enthusiasm. He can dispel apprehension or parry some criticism
in advance by means of a thorough plowing and seeding of ideas.

One advantage of this form over chancel dialogue is that it
does not require extensive study and preparation by the minister. He does not have to slave over a hot typewriter for hours or
engage in endless conferences with a partner-to-be. In fact, since
his formal sermon will be cut down from its usual length or elim-
inated altogether, this approach will probably take much less
study than usual. After all, he is going to do a lot of listening
while many others are sharing the preaching! The pastoral presentation will be just long enough to submit a theme, issue, or
text, and stimulate response from the assembled multitude.

The length of the pastor's introduction will vary with the nature and purpose of the topic. If the pastor wants to make a
statement or submit a text for general discussion and allow the
people to move in any direction, his formal presentation may
take only a minute or two. If he plans to describe a more complex problem or a difficult moral situation, or perhaps read a case
study and then invite comments, his opening statement will be
longer. The general rule seems to be that the more he tries to
narrow and focus the discussion on specific cases or issues, the
longer the pastor's introduction needs to be. If he wants to invite a discussion on faith, for example, his opening statement
might be the text from Hebrews 11:1: "Now faith is the assur-
ance of things hoped for, the conviction of things not seen," or
he might relate the comment of a small boy that "faith is believing something is so when you know it ain't." He could inquire
of the congregation, "Does this statement square with your own
experience?" or "How would you define faith?" The discussion
could move into any one of several directions.

On the other hand, if the pastor wishes to deal with faith in
a specific context he might raise the issue of nuclear war. After
describing the factors that make man's situation today extremely
perilous, he could inquire, "How can a person put his trust in
God and the ultimate victory of his kingdom when the nations
of this world threaten to destroy this world?"

As the minister prepares, he will find it necessary to analyze
his objectives and carefully delineate and define his topic before

he lays it before the congregation. Although there is some value in an open-ended discussion, he will generally want to know where the dialogue is likely to lead. He may not dictate its outcome, but he can certainly impose some limits on it. In any event, his opening statement should be adequate to define the issue but brief enough to provoke discussion and not preclude it.

Even so, the preacher may have difficulty at first in getting his people to open up and speak out without fear of embarrassment, for the average pew-sitter is not used to such goings-on. He is used to just sitting! Until a person's concept of his own role in the worship service is changed, the pastor will find it very difficult to extract thoughts during the discussion period. It may take a very popular issue or a rather upsetting statement to "turn them on." It will be wise for the pastor to prime some individuals in advance for the first few times, asking such persons to be prepared with a question or comment and hoping that others will follow suit when the conversational ball begins bouncing. He will probably find that stimulating discussion is like the comparison made between kissing a girl and getting olives out of the bottle: "After you get the first one, the rest come easy." As people see their peers responding they will be drawn into the communicative happening and, despite their inhibitions, they may find themselves speaking out with feeling and concern. Granted, a complete baring of soul is to be neither expected nor desired in such a context but there may be a depth of sharing that the pastor had not thought possible.

The worship leader will have to steel himself against the embarrassment of silence. Pastors easily panic when there is dead silence! But people need time to reflect and cogitate, and while the wheels are grinding in their heads the pastor will have to hold his tongue even though he may be bursting with his personal opinions. Don't be afraid of silence—the time is not wasted when people are not talking. Quite possibly it is just as important to listen for the voice of God as to talk to each other! After all, the Society of Friends has built its entire worship experience around the economy of silence.

After the worshipers begin speaking to the issue, the pastor will not want to let his thoughts be heard very often, as he might cut off comment from other sources. After all, the people have probably heard his opinions on the subject at hand—this is his golden opportunity to hear theirs! He will not want to interpose a comment after every congregational response, nor respond personally to every question that is raised. Usually it will be more meaningful to allow the people to think through the issues themselves and answer their own questions. One danger inherent in this dialogic approach is that the pastor may pose as an "answerbox" and feel that he must state his point of view every five seconds. There may be times when he will need to clear up some technical question about the Bible or clarify some difficult theological issue, but generally he will maintain a hands-off policy. He will encourage discussion and he will sometimes guide it, but he will not dominate it. Nothing will stifle free expression more easily than a pastor who compulsively out-talks everyone else and forces his opinions on others as if their opinions were worthless or inferior.

Another dangerous tendency is for a few persons in the congregation to take over the discussion, and this is harder to deal with. If the pastor sets the policy of recognizing only those who raise their hands, he will usually be able to recognize a variety of hands and avoid the monopolizing of time by any one person. If he finds it hard to encourage certain ones to speak out, he will prime them with questions beforehand. He will not want to embarrass shy people during the service by directing surprise questions at them. But if he is dealing with a very difficult extrovert who insists on being loquacious, the pastor might make a remark like this: "John, you have made some very fine statements, but I want to see what some others think about this issue. Let me come back to you later." In this case, "later" may mean after the benediction is pronounced!

Another problem is what to do about people who make unkind, scathing, or shocking comments during the discussion. The pastor will have to avoid showing extreme surprise or displeasure, but simply move the discussion in someone else's direction. Let us not underestimate the capacity of the Christian congregation to accept and love each other. Generally the worshiping group is spiritually mature enough to absorb offbeat or angry comments without it becoming a problem. In the process, the redemptive element may become active in the community of faith and it may influence the minds of those who are disturbed.

The pastor may or may not wish to summarize the discussion

at its conclusion. It requires a quick and agile mind to summarize a spontaneous discussion of this kind without overlooking something important or giving stress to the wrong ideas. A good summary is a work of art and a thing of beauty, and it can be very effective as a closing statement to the congregation or as an integral part of the closing prayer. But the pastor must be objective, and that is hard. Let him not make the mistake of closing with his own pet views which are at variance with the general drift of the discussion!

If he is not adept at summaries, the pastor may decide to let the discussion end itself. He will close on a statement which seems to be definitive, provocative, or inspirational. He may say quietly, "This is a good point to stop. We shall proceed with the remainder of our service." Or, "Thank you for your contributions and insights. Let us bow in prayer." Or he may simply pronounce the benediction.

The pastor must resist the temptation to conclude discussion by preaching a sermon. The discussion was the sermon! Nor should he moralize in a manner that betrays the whole discussion, for if it was a meaningful dialogue everyone is now aware that the issue is too complicated to permit simplistic formulas or black-white judgments. It is foolish (and patently dishonest) for the pastor to guide a lengthy discussion on the morality of war and then conclude triumphantly, "Now then: we have all agreed that the God of love cannot sanction the taking of life under any circumstances!" Quite likely no consensus has been reached concerning any phase of that broad topic during the limited time for discussion! The pastor's statement says nothing about the discussion but a great deal about the convictions of the discussion leader. We repeat, however, that a clear, objective summary is a lovely thing and a joy to behold — and a logical and succinct restatement of ideas will enable many people to retain the concepts more easily than they would otherwise.

Finally, we turn to a case study to illustrate what can be done. A Scottish preacher, the Rev. Brian A. Greet, has successfully combined the chancel dialogue and the congregational approaches. His experiment is related in *The Expository Times* of Edinburgh.[3] Mr. Greet began by trying to analyze the purpose and

---

[3] Brian A. Greet, "Dialogue Preaching," *The Expository Times*, Edinburgh, February, 1967.

meaning of holding evening services in his church. He deter-
mined that the evening service should be more than just a pale
repetition of the morning service, that it should allow for mani-
fest congregational participation, and that it should provide
Christian instruction which would enable worshipers to become
more effective Christian apologists. After attempting some innovations in the sanctuary, Mr. Greet decided that such a setting was unsuitable for his more flexible approach. The church
hall proved to be the ideal place, with the kitchen at one end
where refreshments could be provided and chairs in the hall
placed in a crescent formation focusing on a small table which
bore a wooden cross and an open Bible. A lectern was placed
nearby.

Each service took off from a conversational dialogue between
the pastor and a lay person, based on a popularly-phrased topic
like "The Bible Is Out of Date!" After a few moments of platform dialogue, the congregation was involved in the discussion.
The pastor relates enthusiastically that this situation provided
real rapport between speakers and audience, there was a keen
desire to participate, and genuine communication often took
place. Some of Mr. Greet's conclusions give us practical help for
using the congregation-discussion dialogue. He points out that
even the layout of the furniture is important, and if you are
dealing with chairs rather than pews, they may be arranged in a
circular fashion which will suggest a family gathered together
for mutual encouragement and engagement in love. If there is
a choice of locations, the leader should remember that not everyone who speaks out will speak up! It is important that everyone
be able to hear everyone else, without strain.

Mr. Greet suggests that the pastor explain at the outset that
members of the congregation who wish to share in dialogue may
remain seated if they wish. This will encourage timid people to
express themselves without having to rise in full view of everyone. The introductory presentation should not be over-prepared
and it should not take too long. Otherwise the audience may be
awed by the polish of the presentation and regard it as a performance to be watched (or slept through) and discussion will
be inhibited. If one is careful about the way he handles the situation, Mr. Greet says, many benefits will ensue from the regular
use of dialogue preaching.

It may be thought by some that "dialogue preaching" . . . is not preaching at all. I can only reply that if preaching means communicating the Gospel of Jesus Christ, then, most emphatically, this *is* preaching.[4]

The experience of those who have tried it gives evidence that the congregation-discussion method can be a significant aspect of worship and a genuine means of grace and truth for all.

See Chapter 4 of *A Listener's Guide to Preaching*, by William D. Thompson (Nashville: Abingdon Press, 1966), for a complete discussion on preparing the congregation to listen skillfully to preaching.

[4] *Ibid.*, p. 150.

3

DIALOGUE
IN THE CHANCEL

CHANCEL DIALOGUE INVOLVES two or more persons who converse with each other rather than with members of the congregation. Occasionally, the dialogue is staged so that one participant speaks from a position among the worshipers, but his location does not alter the fact that he is part of a carefully planned presentation rather than a spontaneous discussion.

Though the functional relationship between participants is more important than their location, the space they occupy deserves some attention. It is only rarely that the second person speaks from the audience. Even when he does, he does not generally remain there, but he moves up into the chancel area either at the invitation of the preacher or on his own initiative. If the preacher has begun the sermon at the pulpit, the second speaker goes to the lectern, if there is one. If the church's pulpit is in the center, he generally goes there and stands alongside the preacher. Although many dialogue sermons are delivered by two persons who have been seated in the chancel, this doesn't have to be so. One might imagine the second participant to be almost anywhere in the church building: the choir loft, perhaps the balcony, baptistry, or even totally out of sight! One pastor had someone completely hidden speak through a microphone to represent the "Voice of Conscience."

An important concern, aside from content and theme, is that the dialogue participants should be clearly heard. If the nature of the encounter dictates that the participants be somewhere

other than the chancel, adequate attention must be given to ease
of hearing. In a small church, there may be no problem; in a
larger church, electronic amplification may be necessary. If the
second participant is to be seen, the comfort of the audience also
needs to be considered. It may seem clever to put a quasi-angelic
being in the side balcony but it is probably not worth doing if
Monday morning brings sore necks to one-third of the congregation who had craned its collective neck to see the speaker!

The possibility of placing the second speaker out of sight suggests that one may preach a dialogue sermon all by himself. The
Rev. Bruce Brigden, a Presbyterian minister in Cherryvale, Kansas, invited his congregation to discover from Satan himself the
meaning of the phrase, "He descended into Hell." Speaking in
the first person in a distorted voice, he assured the congregation
that God had lied to mankind and that hell is far preferable
to heaven. Midway through the sermon another voice (again Mr.
Brigden's) was heard over the public address system: the words of
Christ refuting the words of Satan. Though only one person's
voice was heard, this was a kind of dialogue sermon due to reasons quite aside from the location of the speaker or the number
of participants. The Rev. Loring D. Chase of the Westmoreland
Congregational Church in Washington, D.C., also preached a
dialogue sermon all alone by the simple expedient of leaning into
the microphone and changing his voice to represent a humorous
and capricious questioner.

What is important in chancel dialogue is that the congregation be caught up in the exchange of ideas and feelings, regardless
of the number of persons involved or their whereabouts.

FUNCTIONS OF CHANCEL DIALOGUE

Just how do the members of the audience get involved in
chancel dialogue? By its very nature, chancel dialogue limits their
involvement to internal, silent participation. In one way, their
activity during a dialogue sermon is the same as it would be
during a traditional, monologue sermon. They may sleep (though
we think they are less likely to!) ; they may hear bits and pieces
in between thoughts of their own; they may put up barriers to
the ideas being proposed; or they may enter creatively into a
dialogue of their own with the preacher by sifting and weighing

his ideas. The advantage of the dialogue sermon is that people are far more likely to identify with what is going on. They will say: "Yes, that's a question I had always wondered about too"; "You're right, don't let him tell you otherwise"; or "I'd like to give that fellow a piece of my mind!"

Certainly the prime purpose of preaching on any subject is to get people to respond. The chancel dialogue psychologically forces the hearer to respond to the view presented at a given moment — perhaps favorably, perhaps not. The hearer may even change his allegiance from side to side, but the well constructed dialogue is designed to (1) help him identify ultimately with the more Christian view, (2) motivate him to further reflection and study in the process of reaching a valid position.

One can never predict with any finality what patterns of thinking or behavior will result from the use of a particular type of dialogue. There seem to be four patterns of chancel dialogue: (1) The dialogue of *support* is essentially a conversation in which the participants discuss a Scripture text or theme on which they share approximately equal knowledge and about which they have similar ideas. The audience identification is largely with the subject itself, although listeners may be attracted to one of the persons involved and tend to follow his line of thinking. (2) The dialogue of *inquiry* poses one participant as a questioner and the other as a resource person. Both are knowledgeable, perceptive, and articulate people but are of uneven sophistication on a particular subject. Generally, the hearer identifies with the questioner, who presumably speaks on behalf of the audience's questions and concerns. (3) The dialogue of *conflict* places the participants in opposition to each other, or to each other's ideas. Here, if the listener has opinions about the subject which were formed previous to the dialogue, he will probably identify with the "good guy." Many listeners, however, may begin listening with an open mind and gradually come to identify with the more persuasive side. (4) A fourth category of chancel dialogue combines these approaches and may add some other elements. We have called this category the *composite* pattern.

PATTERNS OF CHANCEL DIALOGUE

In this section we shall attempt to describe these four patterns which have been used to present dialogue sermons. The method of dialogue preaching, though rooted in antiquity, is still new to our generation. Its value is not established by any long tradition or by empirical studies of effectiveness. Most of the clergymen who have employed this method have done so only once, or a few times at most. Almost without exception, they are enthusiastic about the response to it and eager to experiment some more. Though we have analyzed dozens of dialogue sermons from all parts of the United States and by clergymen of many denominations, we do not present this analysis as the final word on dialogue preaching. At this stage, any analysis is preliminary and tentative.

Certain patterns have emerged, however, from our study. Some of them appear to be eminently worthwhile; others leave some doubt in our minds about their probable effectiveness. The importance of this analysis lies in (1) the reporting of dialogue preaching actually done somewhere by someone, and (2) the suggesting of elements which may be effectively used or combined in new ways by creative readers to facilitate the preaching of the gospel through dialogue.

1. THE DIALOGUE OF SUPPORT

The dialogue of support is conversation. To say this is not to imply that it is dull, spineless, or non-controversial. It is frequently exciting as the participants grapple honestly with some vital issues. When laced with lively language and compelling illustrations, dialogue of support is likely to capture and sustain audience attention as surely as the finest monological sermon or the most exciting debate.

Dialogue between clergy is the number one category, both in the number of sample sermons available and in the ease of composition. Preachers carry on dialogues with each other whenever they get the chance; it is natural for them to carry their conversations into the pulpit.

The first sermon in this book's anthology section, "If I Should Die," is an example of this kind of dialogue. Preached by one of the authors of this book and his pastor, it is an attempt to deal in an unusual way with a rather unusual homiletical subject, the Christian's attitude toward death and funerals. The preachers based their decision to use the dialogical method on the dictum that form follows function. Note Mr. Lightbody's clue to his expectation in the sentence, "Let me raise another rather broad subject that we ought to consider in this setting and discuss in the conversations that we hope you will carry on after this one is concluded." To put it another way, if you want people to engage in dialogue on the sermon topic, provide the impetus by preaching a dialogue sermon!

A topical theme like this one is quite common with supportive clergy dialogues. Other themes in this category are the church's involvement in social issues, a Christian interpretation of sex, the death of God, the new morality, and the social revolution.

The ministers of the First Methodist Church of Germantown, Philadelphia, Pa., preach dialogue sermons frequently. A creative sermon in the supportive category, "Whatever Is Lovely," was preached during an arts festival in the church. The ministers talked of modern art and its meaning, of Keats and Albee and Arthur Miller, of the paintings on display in the church lounge. Most of all, they talked of the apostle Paul's admonition in the letter to the Philippians to think on "whatever is lovely." The Rev. Robert Raines concluded that "art has to do with life — all of life; and all of life has to do with art, all the ways whereby we become whole men in a healed world."

While some dialogues are topical, others tend to deal with traditional themes arising out of biblical passages. In an Advent sermon at St. John's Church (Episcopal) in Waterbury, Conn., the Rev. Peter Holroyd opines that "our task is . . . to find true spiritual values in the real world which surrounds us. Surely this is what the sacraments, baptism, and Holy Communion are supposed to show us." His colleague, the Rev. DeWolf Perry responds, "Exactly so. This is what we are doing in Advent; we are preparing for the coming of God into the world in a very real way." The Lenten themes and passages seem also to lend themselves to dialogical treatment. Pastors George Wilson and James Kirk of St. James Presbyterian Church, San Gabriel, California, preached a series of dialogue sermons during a recent Lenten season. In the beginning of one sermon, "The Dialogue of Lent," Pastor Kirk indicates their purpose for preaching:

> Thus, during this period of Lent, we have returned to this place for renewal. We have returned to hear again and again the word of God, how this word became flesh and how it may have flesh in our everyday lives. Is the word of God alive today?

In the Bushnell Congregational Church of Detroit, Michigan,
Dr. John Forsyth and the Rev. Jeffrey Atwater tackled the question, "Is Christianity the Only True Religion?" While they did
not expound the Bible passage which had been read, Philippians
2:1-11, they did discuss the affirmation of the closing verses which
exalt Christ as Lord of the universe. Their conclusion was that
Christianity is "more true" than other great religions, and that
its Lord, Jesus Christ, "will lead us into all truth."

This same sermon reveals both the strength and weakness of
the supportive dialogue between clergy. Dr. Forsyth begins:

> We have found the process of thinking through our subject quite ex-
> hilarating, and we hope the presentation of our thoughts today will be
> at least interesting to you. This is not to be a debate, for we do not
> stand on opposite sides of the question. It is rather a probing of the
> question, so that you can formulate answers for yourselves, rather than
> to accept final answers from us.

The element of strength is that dialogue speakers do indeed become stimulated by the uniqueness of the method, the necessity
for thorough preparation, and the opportunity to do in public
what they do so well in private — converse on religious questions.
The weakness of this kind of preaching is that it is not intrin-
sically dialogical. One could edit or remove whole chunks of
dialogue, give the preaching responsibility to one preacher, and
not seriously impair the sermon's effectiveness. At one point, for
example, Dr. Forsyth says, "I am in accord with this, and I know
why I believe it. But I would like to know why you believe it."
This is good, honest, human talk. It makes the sermon sound
dialogical. It probably helps to hold the interest of listeners. Its
presence in the sermon, however, is not indispensable to the communication of its message.

Occasionally, one finds a "dialogue" sermon which hardly even
gives the illusion of dialogue. Someone has apparently taken a
traditional monological sermon and has divided the paragraphs
between two speakers. To do this does not make a sermon truly
dialogical.

Dialogue between clergy and laity is a natural outgrowth of the
recent stress in theological writing on the theology of the laity.
It also arises from the rapidly rising educational achievement of
American churchgoers. Persons educated to think for themselves,
to ask penetrating and even embarrassing questions of professors

and other authority figures, are increasingly less likely to be happy with a purely passive role in the church sanctuary. The church's Christian education program for youth and adults has also provoked a proclivity toward vigorous discussion of religious subjects.

One might expect that many clergy-lay sermons would take the form of inquiry or debate; some do, and they will be discussed later. Of interest here is the dialogue sermon in which the layman and his pastor take the role of colleagues. To work in this way is not to cast the layman in the role of clergy; he is himself, but he is sympathetic to the clergyman's point of view on the subject at hand. In one case he may be a foil for the minister's opinions and questions. In another the layman may take the lead, putting his pastor on the spot. The difference between the dialogue of support and the dialogue of inquiry, in this case, is a subtle but real one. Perhaps an examination of the second sermon in the anthology will illustrate the difference.

On the Sunday before Halloween, the Rev. Theodore Whitacre, associate pastor of the Church of the Brethren, Lancaster, Pennsylvania, engaged a college senior on the topic, "The Many Masks of Christians." The minister opened the subject, as one might expect. After only a few lines, however, the layman, David Martin, took the initiative by his assertion, in question form, that "we wear masks all the time." His pastor agreed and opened the way for further observations and questions by the layperson. While the initiative is largely in the layman's hands throughout the sermon, it is passed back and forth enough to keep from casting either person in the role of inquirer or resource person. Although there is occasional disagreement between them on definitions of words, and some friendly sparring, there is no head-on clash of views or personalities. This is clearly a dialogue in which the speakers support each other. Indeed, the concluding sentence is read in unison!

In a sermon entitled "Trust, Don't Try," the Rev. Howard Friend of the Montauk, New York, Community Church, and Mr. Ap Zylstra from Wassenaar, Holland, discussed an Ascensiontide theme. They based it on 1 Corinthians 15:1-11 and developed it in terms of the sufficiency of Christ for every human need. "Life has its problems, doubts, pains, questions, and they're real," concludes Mr. Friend. "But don't try to pull yourself up by your own bootstraps. Don't try to answer all the questions; resolve all the conflicts; heal all the wounds. Repent. Be thankful. Trust, don't try." Like many supportive dialogues, this one might have been given as a monologue. What keeps it dialogical is the richness of illustration brought by each man from his own varied experience.

Dialogue between clergy and youth generally reveals some difference between the outlook of the two generations; even then their stance is roughly the same on a given issue. Most of the sermons in this category handle the expected questions of sex, war, and the movement into adulthood. What is interesting about these sermons as a class is the down-to-earth, everyday language of the youth, the freedom with which they approach their minister, and the flexibility to vary even the dialogue format. In another sermon by the Rev. Theodore Whitacre and an eighteen-year-old youth, the latter suggests, about mid-sermon, that they role-play the conversation between the prodigal son and his older brother after the son's homecoming. After they have done so, they reflect on the meaning of this New Testament story. The pastor begins the interpretation:

Pastor: Don't you see—through this one incident of a boy leaving home the family was finally brought together again. If we work toward the reuniting of the generations, maybe some day we shall be reconciled as they were.

Youth: Would that all adults would have the compassion and love for their sons and daughters that this man of whom Jesus spoke in his parable had for his!

The young person then concludes by reading a modern language translation of Jesus' parable and, with some concluding hopes expressed, the sermon ends.

One clergy-youth sermon which deals with a traditional subject in a unique format was preached at the Westminster Presbyterian Church of Portland, Oregon, by the pastor, the Rev. Robert H. Bonthius, and his son, Robert, Jr. It starts:

Pastor: This is Youth Sunday. It has been the practice in our congregation to welcome youth to leadership in the services. This we do today. What is unusual is to find that one of these youth is one of my sons! The Youth Work Committee apparently thought it had the makings of a lively dialogue when it suggested that Bob Jr. participate in the interpretation of the Word with me.

Bob: It came as quite a shock to me—the idea that I would have to *communicate* with my father. Or, for that matter, with any adult.

Pastor: Yes, I recall your mother telling me recently that she had mentioned this dialogue coming up, and you said, "Boy, Dad and I had better start talking!" I think we've done well so far; getting this sermon prepared has involved a goodly number of hours. And you finished the study book for Youth Week before I did. Did you find it fairly down to earth?

Bob: Yes, I did find the book down to earth, because it dealt not in *abstract* terms, but in *concrete* terms with idols which youth worship today instead of Christ.

The family team continues with an exposition of modern idols and the power of Christ to dethrone these powers and put them in their place. The sermon concludes:

Pastor: Thanks, Bob, for joining me in this dialogue.

Bob: Yes, and I do hope we can talk again before I go off to college!

Dialogue between faiths is an increasingly popular form of pulpit address in the emerging ecumenical spirit of the age. As both Protestant and Roman Catholic groups come together for Week of Christian Unity services, Reformation Day worship, Brotherhood Week events, and other interfaith gatherings, clergy of both faiths are experimenting with dialogue preaching.

It is indicative of the spirit in which these meetings are held that the interfaith dialogue sermons we have seen are supportive. In some inquiry dialogues, one clergyman is a guest in the pulpit of another church. In that setting, he is the resource person. There may well be some dialogues of conflict too, but these are not so common. When Protestant and Catholic groups come together for worship or fellowship, they seem to explore areas of agreement, to confess the sin of having divided the body of Christ, and to seek ways of implementing the unity they find in Jesus Christ. They also point out the honest differences which still divide Christendom.

In the sermon "The Unity We Seek," by Pastor Robert Bonthius and Father Waldschmidt of Portland, Oregon, a warm spirit of brotherhood in Christ is apparent. The setting is Reformation Sunday, an occasion in many Protestant churches for celebrating the separation from Catholicism in the sixteenth century. In this sermon, the men have achieved a remarkable balance between the expression of difference and the hope for a reformation that is yet to come. The sermon is laced with personal references and good humor. It is strongly historical and

theological, but the level of its language is understandable only
to a congregation of above-average education.

Pastor Bonthius also preached a dialogue sermon on "The
Death of Jesus" with Rabbi Emanuel Rose of Portland's Congregation Beth Israel. Rabbi Rose observed that probably "this is
the first pulpit dialogue of its kind," and he went on to raise the
question on which the rest of the sermon pivots: "Why does
Christianity place such an overriding importance and significance
on the death of Jesus?" From his insights concerning Judaism at
the time of Jesus, he added a great store of information concerning the circumstances surrounding Jesus' death. Pastor Bonthius
responded to the rabbi's questions about Christian anti-Semitism
with the confession that Christians' rejection of any man is a
means by which they participate in the death of Christ. He concluded, "Only as we Christians come to see the connection between love of God made known in Christ and love that extends
itself in costly service to all his earthly brothers, will we stop
the crucifixion of Jesus."

One might consider this dialogue one of conflict, since the two
speakers disagree theologically. It is included in this section,
however, because there is no real clash of opinions; nor is one
speaker just an inquirer. Both move forward, probing, question-
ing, clarifying, and supporting each other's aim to understand for
himself and his tradition the meaning of Jesus' death.

2. THE DIALOGUE OF INQUIRY

Relatively few dialogue sermons which we have examined fall
into the category of inquiry, in which the participants perform
well-defined roles as inquirer and resource person. Perhaps the
best way to describe this type is to quote from a dialogue presentation given at the First Christian Church of Alva, Oklahoma.
The Rev. James Gentle and the Rev. Richard Hendricks chose
the topic "The Will of God." Mr. Gentle said in his introduction:

> To proclaim the good news we think there are a variety of forms which
> should be used. Twentieth-century Protestantism has, too often, reduced
> its preaching to clergymen, who stand in black robes, in a particular
> pulpit on Sunday morning, using funny sounding words, talking about
> irrelevant principles. We believe that proclamation—preaching—should
> use a variety of forms—movies, records, filmstrips, drama, lectures, songs,
> anthems, small-group conversations, and dialogue.

Dialogue is far more than two people talking TO each other; it is two people talking WITH one another. We must listen. We must be present. We must seek to be open. Instead of preparing our own argument, we must listen to what the other person is saying.

We will assume the roles as "inquirer" and "respondent." One will introduce into the dialogue questions, beliefs, and interpretations which are common and reflect our uncertainty of the teachings of the church. The other will respond, to which the first may continue to raise questions of clarification.

This approach was unique because of the attempt to open the possibility of congregational involvement, for Mr. Gentle went on to tell the congregation to write out their questions on little slips of paper and pass them up to the "Inquirer" during the dialogue, who would include them in his conversation with the "Respondent." Even though this was ostensibly a chancel dialogue involving two persons, there were far more than two participants if indeed the worshipers did raise questions that were included in the presentation.

There is no evidence in the sermon that such questions were presented and handled on the spot. However, in their dialogues of the next two Sundays the ministers referred to questions that had been submitted. Though much of this dialogue could be labeled "supportive," Mr. Gentle generally carried the role of resource person, using very specific illustrations from contemporary life and the Scriptures to deal with the questions raised by the inquirer.

Another approach to dialogues of inquiry involves the clergy-laity axis. The Rev. Dr. John W. McKelvey of St. Anthony Park Methodist Church, St. Paul, Minnesota, preached at least two such sermons. One involved his lay leader, Dr. William Hartwick; the other, a member of the official board, Mr. Robert D. Munson. Evidently Dr. McKelvey did not warn his congregation that a layman would share in the sermon, nor did he indicate the roles to his congregation; but those roles became quite obvious as the sermon developed. Both laymen had the one function of asking questions. The dialogue with Dr. Hartwick began with the pastor's statement that evil is evident in our world in many forms. Dr. Hartwick responded:

Worshiper: What you are saying, sir, is certainly true, but to me what is even more appalling is that evil should be present at all, let alone run rampant in the world about us. If God is our

Creator and Ruler, how do you explain this endless tyranny of evil?

Preacher: You have asked the crucial question when you demand an explanation of evil in a world created by a good God and called "good" by the Creator Himself. Perhaps the best way of arriving at an answer is to explore the different kinds of evil in order to be sure we are talking about the same thing.

Worshiper: But, Mr. Preacher, isn't evil just what it implies, evil? What difference can there be when you are up against evil?

Preacher: Well, there are differences. There are "natural" and "human" evils, or to make a better distinction, "manageable" and "unmanageable evils." Let me take a moment to explain the point of this distinction.

Not only is the role of the inquirer clear by the fact that he is always asking questions, but he is constantly addressing his pastor as "Mr. Preacher" or "Sir." This form of address appears artificial, and perhaps a bit condescending. It may have reflected the real relationship between the two men; or they may have thought it necessary to keep the roles clear in this way, but the language in this sermon is anything but natural and authentic.

Dialogues of inquiry between clergy and youth represent another type. Shortly after the Blake-Pike proposal was launched in San Francisco, the Rev. Myron Hall, minister of the Jason Lee Memorial Methodist Church of Salem, Oregon, preached a dialogue sermon with a young Methodist at the Oregon Conference District Youth Conference. This dialogue captures the kind of conversation that is human and real:

Youth: Do you have a minute?

Adult: If it's important, I have a minute.

Youth: It's important to me.

Adult: Then it's important to me. What is it?

Youth: It's about something I read in the paper recently. At some big church meeting, somebody proposed that the churches ought to unite.

Adult: You mean the proposal made last December at the meeting of the National Council of Churches? Eugene Carson Blake, who holds the highest office possible in the Presbyterian Church, proposed that the Methodist Church, The Protestant Episcopal Church, The Presbyterian Church and the United Church of Christ—the new name for the Congregational Church—ought to unite.

Youth: Yes, that's it.

Adult: Well, what about it?

Youth: I think it's a wonderful idea.

The dialogue goes on to cover some of the thoughts and queries of the young person concerning the ecumenical movement. Like real conversation, most of the speeches in the dialogue are short, pithy, and to the point. The questions and responses of the youth really sound like a young person: the adult sounds like a mature, warm, understanding adult.

Two Episcopal clergymen have published a collection of sermons which are dialogues of inquiry.[1] In 1953, the Rev. George W. Barrett and the Rev. J. V. Langmead Casserley preached a series of four Advent sermons at New York's historic Trinity Church. Based on eschatological themes, the sermons were edited for publication to sound more like an interview in the rector's study than a pulpit presentation. In actual preaching, one clergyman assumed the role of the inquiring layman.

Two Roman Catholic priests in St. Louis, Fathers John Patrick Daly and Francis J. Matthews, gave a series of Lenten dialogue sermons of inquiry at St. Michael's parish in Shrewsbury, a suburban community. Their purpose was very timely and practical: to help the rather conservative members of that parish understand and appreciate the sweeping changes taking place in the Catholic Church in the period following Vatican II. Reported in Father Daly's master's thesis, "Dialogue Preaching: A Technique for Effecting Change," [2] the series featured Father Matthews as the "expert" on the theology of change and Father Daly as a bewildered, inquiring Catholic layperson who wanted to know exactly why the precious, traditional liturgy and dogma of his Church was being suddenly reviewed and revised so drastically. The dialogues were written in the vernacular and a great effort was made to have Father Daly raise questions that were really "bugging" the people of that parish.

In spite of the artificiality of a priest's representing the layman's point of view, the congregation's response to a questionnaire indicated an overwhelming appreciation for the series. Eighty persons said that they felt well represented by the questioner; three did not. Seventy-three felt they had a better idea

---

[1] George W. Barrett and J. V. Langmead Casserley, *Dialogue on Destiny* (New York: The Seabury Press, Inc., 1955).

[2] John Patrick Daly, *Dialogue Preaching: A Technique for Effecting Change.* Unpublished Master's thesis, graduate school of St. Louis University, St. Louis, Mo., 1966.

of what it means to be a Catholic as a result of the dialogue;
eight did not. The questions designed to measure the degree of
attitude change were not sophisticated enough to produce a valid
judgment about the effect of the dialogues in changing people's
minds about the issues in question, but there was indication that
changes in Catholic liturgy and policy were accepted much more
readily than if the series had not been presented. Here is a case
where dialogue of inquiry was very useful as an educational and
persuasive tool, if we can believe the evaluation of those involved in it. Also significant was the congregation's answer to the
question, "Would you like to see the dialogue technique used in
place of Sunday sermons periodically?" Eighty out of eighty-three
persons responded affirmatively. Even if we can't prove that the
series fully sold the congregation on the innovations in Roman
Catholic worship and policy, it certainly sold them on the use of
dialogue as a homiletical device!

The inquiry sermon chosen for the anthology section of this
book has an interesting twist. The minister, who began by
preaching on Abraham's trek to the Holy Land, was interrupted
by a stranger — actually a new member of the church who was a
Negro minister involved in chaplaincy work. The pastor, the
Rev. Robert Bolton, made the point that Abraham tried to solve
his problems by evasion and that this solution is not possible in
our kind of society. After noting that reconciliation is the message of the New Testament, the stranger, the Rev. Harlan London, interrupted to establish the parallel between biblical and
contemporary society, and to ask the minister to get down to
cases. Mr. London then became the resource person and Mr.
Bolton the inquirer: a role reversal had taken place. The interrupter ended the sermon affirming a Christian hope for a new
society, having thoughtfully fulfilled his job of resource person.

There are dangers in working with these three kinds of inquiry: clergy-clergy, clergy-layman, and clergy-youth. Inquiry can
easily degenerate into artificiality or condescension, and it can
become "stagy" or theatrical. In the ideal form of inquiry, each
partner is a responsible participant who happens to have authentic questions or some thoughtful answers on the subject at hand.
He will exercise his responsibility of inquirer or resource person
in language that is human, accurate, and clear to the audience at
large.

3. THE DIALOGUE OF CONFLICT

By using the term "conflict" we do not mean to suggest unpleasantness, acrimony, or outspoken hostility. Conflict here denotes opposing ideas represented by persons who may be quite friendly. The participants in a dialogue of conflict will disagree, perhaps vehemently, certainly vigorously, on the issue before them; they are not necessarily disagreeable.

One might expect this kind of dialogue to be a simple debate: two persons, lay or clergy, taking opposite sides. In actuality, the dialogue of conflict takes a wide variety of styles. The opposing forces are seldom two persons speaking only for themselves; more often they are representatives of a point of view. More than the dialogues of support or inquiry, the dialogue of conflict is drama. Because of this strong dramatic element, congregations generally need some preparation for listening or sharing in it. In some sophisticated congregations — those in a university setting, for example — people may be accustomed to unusual presentations; in other situations the unorthodox must be carefully introduced. In most churches where such dialogues have been preached, an announcement has been made in the parish paper or from the pulpit a week or more in advance of the presentation. Occasionally, the warning that something unusual is coming is built into the sermon's introduction.

In a dialogue presented at a gathering of the United Campus Christian Fellowship at the University of Nebraska, the Rev. Hudson B. Phillips introduced his colleague and the method of preaching at the same time:

> This morning Alan Pickering and I will present our topic in the form of a "Dialogue Sermon." It is named this way because we will be speaking to each other as well as to you, in order to make more graphic the point that every sermon is really a kind of conversation between friends about the nature of our corporate ministry.
>
> The dialogue sermon form is very old. It originated in the Fifth Century in the famous Greek Schools of Philosophy—sometimes called the "peripatetic" schools, because those who belonged to them used to walk about the gardens and groves of Academe, conversing and discussing together the meaning of life. . . . The dialogue form had only limited value in ancient Greece, however, and it had to wait until the Middle Ages before it achieved real fame and fortune. At that time, it became a popular form of teaching and exhortation, because it was so easily adaptable to evangelistic purposes. With both a positive and a negative

side, the sermons were always prepared so that the good guys won. And in fact, that will be the case with today's sermon as well, but largely because of my superior presentation and eloquent delivery.

Yes, dialogue lends itself to sarcasm and other forms of humor!

Now we shall examine the various types of conflict dialogue. It would have been possible to have combined them into two or three general categories; instead categories were invented for nearly every dialogue of conflict for which an example could be found. This was done so that the reader who wishes to attempt dialogue preaching may have the widest possible set of options from which to choose (or depart).

Advocatus Diaboli — Vindicatus Dei: An example of this approach has already been suggested. The subject of the sermon by Mr. Pickering and Mr. Phillips was "Is God Dead?" One might think from Mr. Phillips' introduction that the sermon would end with a ringing affirmation that God is indeed alive. Actually, it concludes with this doleful statement by the "Advocatus Diaboli," Mr. Pickering:

> So rest in peace, God. You were great while you were here, but you were smart to quit while you were ahead. Let the Lucifer League take over now, and if people don't like our way better, you'll be the first to know. That's because we always use your name when we swear, and so you'll know from the cussing just how we're getting on now that you've gone.
> God is alive? The Hell you say! God is dead!

Mr. Phillips' prediction that the "good guys" would emerge victorious is fulfilled only in the minds of the listeners who, presumably, have seen through the weak arguments of the devil's advocate.

There are many variations of this technique. The dialogue sermons of this type seem generally to be breezy, filled with sharp figures of speech, and wryly humorous. Perhaps this is because no one takes the concept of a personal devil very seriously; or, possibly, the idea is so frightening that one must invoke a sense of humor to live with it.

Christ and Satan: We have one example of a dialogue sermon which pits Satan against Christ. It is the sermon to which we have already alluded by the Rev. Bruce Brigden of Cherryvale, Kansas. After establishing his identity as Satan and the location as Hell, Mr. Brigden continues speaking in the voice of Satan: "Do we meet at last, O mine enemy?" By means of a tape recording played over the public address system, the same man's voice is used to represent Christ: "We meet again, Brother Satan."

Satan: And this time, it is on my terms. But how did you fall? Who stole your life, when I could not?

Christ: No man took it from me. I laid it down for a friend. I have followed my brothers where they have gone, that they might follow me where I shall go.

Satan: Once again you are wrong! None but the dead can enter here, and none but the living can escape.

Christ: I have laid down my life, and I can take it up again. And now, let my people go, that those who love light more than darkness may receive their true reward.

Satan: I'll stop you. I am the Lord here. (Light comes on.) Oh, the brightness!

In the dialogue which follows, Satan is conquered by the resurrection power of Christ, and the congregation concludes the service with the singing of the hymn, "Christ the Lord Is Risen Today."

Clergy and Layman: On a recent Easter Sunday, Dr. Ralph Ely, a layman at First Presbyterian Church of Durham, North Carolina, interrupted his pastor, the Rev. David Currie, with "Mr. Currie, please excuse my interrupting, but why must you preach *only* of the resurrection on Easter?" After summoning the layman to the pulpit, Mr. Currie defended his choice of sermon topic. As the dialogue continued, it became apparent that the layman wanted a topic which was more life-centered, more here-and-now. Near the conclusion of the dialogue Dr. Ely says:

Layman: Preacher, you were starting out today to emphasize the resurrection and I objected—objected because it seemed to me that emphasis on the resurrection was escapist, was irrelevant, was speculation. I wanted you to claim the opportunity of Easter to declare the responsibility of Christians for bold and faithful actions in this present life. But I am beginning to see some direct connection between faith in the resurrection and Christlike actions on our part. . . . I can see that the resurrection is not an ancillary part of Christian life or faith.

Pastor: And you have helpfully reminded me that the resurrection alone is not the climactic, mysterious conclusion of Christian faith, irrelevant to Christian action and life.

Layman: Well, I hope that you will forgive my interruption.

Clergy: Assuredly—and please accept my thanks for your help. Let us all, once again, hear the text: [1 Corinthians 15:54b-58].

Clergy and Youth: The Rev. Wayne H. Keller, of the South-minster Presbyterian Church in Seattle, Washington, drew upon material published by the National Council of Churches to deal with the subject of sex. The booklet "Called to Responsible Freedom" formed the basis of his dialogue with a young person. The dialogue opens in a sprightly, breezy manner:

Youth: Responsible freedom? There they go again. These church guys are really something. They tell us they want us to be free, which sounds real cool, but just try really being free and they lower that big boom they call responsibility. They pull this act all the time in committee meetings to plan parties, in discussion groups of every kind, and now they are trying to sell us their pitch about sex. How simple do they think we are? If we are going to be free in our dating, then, man, let us be free! Don't give us that responsible business! We don't mind being told what we should and shouldn't do (of course we may not pay any attention to such advice), but don't try to pretend that this means freedom. We know that you can't have your cake and eat it too, so stop trying to persuade us that we can.

Clergy: Touche, my friend. There's truth in what you say, but lend me your ears for a few minutes, will you please? I know you are confused about this business of sex, and I admit that we church guys, as you call us, are partly to blame. But that's what this program is all about. We are trying to bring a little light into what is a pretty dark room.

The clergyman goes on to admit that his generation has been responsible for much of the misplaced emphasis on sex, the lack of adequate education, the hypocrisy of the adult world. He then calls the youth's attention to the biblical concern with sex in particular and with morality in general. The Pharisees come under his judgment as persons who

Clergy: Would have your relationships with the opposite sex regulated totally. . . . You could neck in a parked car for six minutes and thirty seconds, but no longer, and there would be carefully detailed rules about what you could and could not do. Precious little freedom, is there?

Youth: Are you kidding??????

Clergy: Well, both Jesus and the Apostle Paul were seeking to set men free from this sort of legalistic bondage. . . . Against this viewpoint, Jesus argued that it meant very little merely to refrain from doing wrong outwardly while inwardly one was seething with illicit desires, or to do the right thing grudgingly and reluctantly. . . . The man who really loves God and his neighbor doesn't need any laws or rules to tell him what to do or not to do. He spon-

Youth: taneously and freely and joyously acts out of love. . . . Now that's what we mean by freedom.

Youth: Yeah, but isn't that kind of dangerous? To let people do as they please seems—well, you know, dangerous!

Clergy: Of course it is! Freedom is always dangerous.

Mr. Keller and his young friend go on to discuss the implications of the tenuous relationship between freedom and responsibility. The young person reacts briefly and incisively with questions that establish points of conflict and give opportunity for the pastor's response. The dialogue concludes:

Youth: Well, I'm not sure that you've sold me, but you sure have given me a lot to think about. Do you mind if I mull this over for a bit and talk about it with some other people?

Clergy: My friend, I would mind very much if you didn't do just exactly that . . . [This dialogue] is intended simply to serve as a springboard for your further thought and discussion from which you can leap into the pool of personal decision. From here on, the matter is between you and the Lord.[3]

Clergy and Skeptic: In this category we are letting "skeptic" stand for a variety of forces or ideas which stand contrary to Christian affirmations. In one instance the skeptic is represented as "the world," which interrupts a service of Holy Communion to say, "I am the hungry bleeding world. I represent countless millions of people who do not understand what you are doing here." When he is asked what he wants, he replies, "I want an explanation! How can you partake of this bread when the world is full of hungry people, people who have not crumbs or crust to eat?" The minister who is conducting the service parries with "the world" for several paragraphs of dialogue, then leads the congregation in partaking of the elements in a contrite spirit. This dialogue was presented by the ministers of the First Baptist Church of Ottawa, Kansas, the Rev. Dr. Raymond P. Jennings and the Rev. Robert E. Sherbondy.[4]

Another clergy-skeptic dialogue of conflict was written by the Rev. Gordon Bennett and preached with the Rev. D. Richard

[3] Excerpts from "Called to Responsible Freedom" by William Graham Cole. Published for The United Christian Youth Movement. Copyright © 1961 by the National Council of the Churches of Christ in the U.S.A. Used by permission.

[4] Raymond P. Jennings and Robert E. Sherbondy, "Communion in Dialogue," *Church Management*, March, 1965, pp. 18-19.

Hepler. Its title, "I Resolve," is suggested both by the season of the year and the sermon subject. The pastor begins with a poem about the opportunities the new year offers, and then suggests what some of his personal resolutions are for the new year. From the far corner of the sanctuary comes a voice:

Voice: Hold on there! You preachers are all alike.

Clergy: What do you mean, "all alike?" What kind of a statement is that? Who are you, anyway?

Voice: I am nobody and I am every man. I am the average person of the world. I am the disillusioned person everywhere: the maimed, the downtrodden, the disappointed zealot of Jesus' time, the serf of the Middle Ages, the discontented peasant of history, the oppressed, huddled masses of starving humanity today. I speak for these people. And I say that you preachers are all alike because you are. You reel off nice-sounding platitudes each year as resolutions for your people. Then you have to repeat them the following January because you never made any progress.

Clergy: Huh?

The Voice continues his tirade against the church and her shortcomings. At the conclusion of the encounter, the minister has evidently learned how far short the church really is — and the extent of his own hypocrisy — and he completely recasts his resolutions for the new year. The skeptic — everyman — reminds the pastor of the apostle Paul's resolution to "press on toward the goal for the prize of the upward call of God in Christ Jesus." The minister responds:

Clergy: Thank you, sir, for your interruption this morning. You may go back and tell your people that from now on the Christian church, this one anyway, will make stronger resolutions. Resolutions so big they'll make us want to grow bigger. For Christ's sake.

Another preacher-skeptic sermon is "Preacher Meets Hippie," by the Rev. D. Richard Hepler. Presented to a congregation of predominantly younger people (ages 8-16), it had a strongly dramatic flavor because of the garb of the two participants. The preacher wore a clerical robe; the hippie wore attire appropriate to his way of life. Neither character was out to convert the other; they opened up the issue: What are the ingredients of love?

Another sermon in this category is unusual in that it combines the preacher-skeptic encounter with three situation-dialogues or dramatic skits. The question "Who Believes in Miracles?" which is the title of the sermon by Gordon Bennett is posed by the skeptic, and the pastor attempts to deal with it not only with argument but also with the experience of three persons in the church or community. In the center of the platform are two chairs; on either side are the two speakers' stands. After the initial dialogue-encounter, the pastor slips over to the central area where he talks with (a) a layman who is brought to his senses and to Christ as he is confronted with his own moral weakness, (b) a layman whose psychosomatic illness is cured when he comes to terms with himself in his hospital room, and (c) a church lay leader who reflects on the miraculous change in the life of a parish after its building burned. At the close, the skeptic is nearly convinced of the possibilities of modern miracles.

Biblical Characters: The Bible is filled with conversations between people, written to communicate the gospel. Church-produced dramas have used this method widely. One dialogue sermon recreates a conversation between John the brother of James, and his father, Zebedee. Zebedee begins by musing on his life, his gift of two fine sons, and his bewilderment that one of them should follow a wandering prophet, Jesus of Nazareth. His question to John, "My son, what has come over you?" gives John the motive for telling about Jesus and his offer of eternal life.

One might construct similar conversations between other biblical characters: David and Saul, Jesus and Lazarus, Luke and Silas. In most congregations, it might be desirable to inform the congregation that such dialogues are hypothetical. A few biblical conversations, however, are recorded in such completeness that they could be read in their entirety, possibly followed by an interpretation.

Prophet and Professor: Pitting an Old Testament-type prophet against a college professor of religion is a way of sharpening the issues in contemporary Christian practice. This situation occurs in the sermon "The Prophet and the Professor" by Gordon Bennett. The opening lines will suggest the flavor of the sermon.

Prophet: Repent, lest ye perish! I bring tidings of doom to a sinful, proud nation. You who turn your backs on God, you who worship the creature and not the creator, you who flaunt your sins before the Almighty, hear this word of warning: stop while there is time. Repent, lest ye perish. . . .

Professor: I say, Mr. Prophet, sir!

Prophet: You who demean marriage and defile your offspring, you who deny the Lordship of Christ. . . .

Professor: Excuse me, please.
Prophet: You who proclaim that all is relative, you who disclaim the
moral imperatives and deny the commandments of God Almighty, I say this to you: repent, lest ye perish!
Professor: Stop that foolishness, prophet!

The conversation moves rapidly into a debate in which the professor attempts to persuade the prophet not to be so extreme. The prophet is unmovable in his position, and unquenchable in his enthusiasm for his cause. At the close, the prophet ascends to a climax in his plea for godliness and social righteousness, and the professor sits down, exhausted and defeated.

Alter Ego: The Rev. Loring D. Chase, minister of the West-moreland Congregational Church of Washington, D.C., was referred to earlier in this chapter. He preached an Advent sermon in which his alter ego, or voice of conscience, carried on a dialogue with him. Both voices were his; he leaned into the microphone and changed the pitch of his voice for the alter ego voice:

Pastor: As Christmas began its approach, back in September or October,
I found myself faced with this question:
Voice: What're you going to read on Christmas Eve this year? Last
year you read American poetry. The year before you read British
poetry. Going to branch out into a different language this year?
Pastor: No, English is tough enough. But I think I'll go back to the
words of Christian geniuses of earlier centuries and of different
cultures and see what they have had to say about the meaning
of Christmas as they have thought about the mystery and the
wonder of the birth of the child Jesus.
Voice: They wrote in English?
Pastor: No, but their words have been translated into English.

Mr. Chase quotes some lines from Athanasius' oration "On the Incarnation of the Word" which becomes the subject for the remaining minutes of the dialogue.

One might consider the alter ego to be an example of the dialogue of support; it represents, however, a prod, a sharp stick, a jarring note in what would otherwise be a monologue.

Ins and Outs: The second dialogue of conflict in the anthology section was preached at the Peoples Presbyterian Church of Milan, Michigan by the pastor, the Rev. Vern R. Campbell, and an elder, Mr. Fred Libbey. The sermon's introduction makes clear that the two participants represent the good and the bad, the sheep and the goats, the "ins" and the "outs" of society. Built on Jesus' parable of the last judgment in Matthew 25:31-46, the voice of the "outs" responds to each phrase voiced by the King in praise of those on his right hand.

Trialogue: The word "trialogue" has already been defined as a dialogue sermon in which three persons, or voices, are used. Every trialogue examined by the authors is in the category of the dialogue of conflict. The reason is probably that, in most trialogues, a tension is set up around a central figure who is trying either to select alternatives or to mediate a dispute. Even when the three persons function in other ways, they are grappling with some issue.

One trialogue has been chosen for the anthology section of the book, to suggest how at least one group of three or more persons might present a sermon which has a dialogical stance. Other combinations of persons or characters that have appeared in trialogue sermons are as follows:

1. The sermon, "Don't Blame God," presented by the Rev. Howard E. Friend, Jr., and five airmen from a nearby military base. Perhaps we should call it a "multilogue" sermon. The minister read the Twenty-third Psalm, a phrase at a time. Responding to the reading were three persons: a devil's advocate, a worshiper seeking some insight into the Scripture despite the devil, and another worshiper who was sympathetic to the devil but who had ambivalent feelings about what he heard.

2. Three young people of the Calvary Baptist Church in Norristown, Pennsylvania, preached a trialogue which began with a teen-ager in despair over her generation. A young man stood up in the congregation shouting, "Wait a minute!" He made his way to the pulpit to defend his generation. Together, they decided to summon another girl who came forward to mediate the dispute and to sum it up.

3. Fathers Paul Goodland and Douglas Haviland of St. John's by the Campus (Episcopal) in Ames, Iowa, preached a Lenten series on the seven deadly sins. Using an allegorical approach, they articulated the attitude toward each of the sins which might be taken by Mr. Natural Man, Mr. Straight and Narrow, and Mr. Christian.

4. Three students at Colgate Rochester Divinity School presented a chapel service in which the first speaker represented, roughly, a neoorthodox position; the second speaker a liberal position; and the third speaker, a robed figure in the pulpit, the

Word of God. The first two speakers spoke casually, hesitantly. The figure in the pulpit spoke with authority, gradually winning each of the other two to a biblical position. This sermon appears in its entirety in an issue of *The Pulpit*.[5]

5. An Episcopal church in New York City featured a trialogue preached about building lavish and expensive churches. One speaker spoke out strongly for the traditional Episcopal position; one spoke for the store-front approach; the third sought to combine the best of both and gave examples of European churches that combined low cost with beauty and functional value.

6. Several examples of the everyman-type who is the object of competition between God and Satan can be found in *Man in the Middle*,[6] a published collection of trialogues. Its authors are Canon Howard Johnson and Bishop James Pike, who were on the staff of the Cathedral of St. John the Divine in New York City when the sermons were preached. These are thoughtful, stimulating, and witty treatments of each of the seven deadly sins.

7. The Rev. John D. Banks, pastor of the Bethany Congregational Church of Quincy, Massachusetts, has preached several trialogues with his associate pastors. In one, "What is the Meaning of Life?" the Christian Realist, in clerical garb, is in conversation with the Moral Philosopher, in street clothes. They are discussing the general malaise of American culture when they are interrupted by the Secular Existentialist, dressed in shabby garb, who is rushing up to the chancel from the congregation. In another sermon the minister reads the Scripture, Jeremiah 38:17-23, and comments that Jeremiah's counsel to surrender to Babylon was probably unwise. A man named Jeremy stamps down the center aisle to defend the counsel that a nation should trust in God rather than military might. He, in turn, is interrupted by a secularist who takes a militant position. In this sermon, the minister finally becomes the mediator.

8. A Lutheran minister, the Rev. Paul F. Keller of Minneapolis, Minnesota, has collaborated with Mr. Stan Kloth in the

[5] John E. Skoglund and David Matteson, "Making Dialogue Preach," *The Pulpit*, August, 1961, pp. 8-9.

[6] James A. Pike and Howard A. Johnson, *Man in the Middle* (Greenwich, Conn.: The Seabury Press, Inc., 1956).

preparation of "For the Sake of the People," [7] a dialogue sermon-drama in six parts. A product of Kairos Publications, a business firm to provide "working tools for parish renewal," this dialogue series was prepared for weekly use during the six weeks of Lent. Mr. Smith is an inquisitor who attempts to discover why Mr. Jones has taken certain unorthodox positions about peace, protests, violence, and other controversial issues. A moderator introduces, concludes, and summarizes. A well-written trialogue that incisively attacks the issue of the Christian's approach to war, this "sermon-drama" can be produced even more effectively with such accompanying materials as litanies which can be used in the worship setting, promotional materials, and specially designed paraments to enrich the context of worship. A slide set which is used during the dialogue as an exhibit-in-evidence is made available with purchase of the basic package.

9. Thomas Kane, a first-year theology student at Philadelphia's St. Charles Borromeo Seminary, used a brief motion picture entitled "Very Nice, Very Nice" to introduce the theme of superficiality and meaninglessness in modern American culture. He followed the film with a brief biblical exposition of 1 Thessalonians 5:1-11 on the importance of a deep Christian faith, and he asked the congregation to reflect upon the meaning of what they had seen and heard. More specifically, he asked them to divide into buzz groups of six or eight persons and be ready to report in precise terms what difference they thought this presentation might make in their lives. Then he chose two or three groups to report, and followed it with a final challenge. This sermon is not a trialogue like the others we have just discussed, but we mention it because it illustrates another approach. It is a trialogue presentation, broadly defined, in that it included interaction between priest, film, and congregation.

The use of motion picture films and other visual aids to stimulate and communicate meaning is growing rapidly, and such techniques are often made a part of public worship or the Christian education program. Those who utilize these media frequently involve the audience in verbal dialogue as well. The following resources are suggested for those who wish to pursue this avenue:

[7] Paul Keller and Stan Kloth, *For the Sake of the People* (Minneapolis, Minn.: Kairos Publications, 1968).

Catholic Film Newsletter, and a *Guide to Current Films,* each published once a month, by the National Catholic Office for Motion Pictures, 453 Madison Ave., New York, N.Y. 10022. ($5.00)

William Jones, *Sunday Night at the Movies,* Richmond, Va., John Knox Press. ($1.95)

Patrick J. McCaffrey, *Films for Religious Education* and *Films for Religious Education II,* Notre Dame, Indiana, Fides Publishers, Inc. ($1.25)

Sister Bede Sullivan, O.S.B., *Movies, Universal Language,* Notre Dame, Indiana, Fides Publishers, Inc. ($2.45)

4. COMPOSITE PATTERNS OF DIALOGUE PREACHING

Although most of the dialogue preaching that has been done falls neatly into our three categories of support, inquiry, and conflict, some of it cannot be understood except as a combination or modification of these three basic approaches.

The Rev. Howard Friend, of the Montauk Community Church, New York, has composed a fascinating Advent sermon, "The Politics of Power and the Promise of Peace." The sermon is divided into three parts which deal with the relationship of the promise of peace to (1) international tensions, (2) the glorification of violence, and (3) the potential for love. Reader One opens each section with a passage of Scripture appropriate to that division of thought. Reader Two follows with contemporary writing: newspaper stories which illustrate international tensions, sentences from Ian Fleming's James Bond novels to illustrate the glorification of violence, news articles about human goodness in the midst of tragedy to illustrate the potential for love. Threaded throughout the sermon are comments from Reader Three which interpret the contrasting readings, and put them in Christian perspective. Here is an extract:

First Reader: And Jesus said, "Love your enemies, bless them that persecute you."

Second Reader: "The finger stood upright, away from the hand, then started to bend slowly backwards toward his wrist. Suddenly it gave. There was a sharp crack. . . . Bond uttered a soft animal groan and fainted."[8]

[8] Ian Fleming, *Live and Let Die* in *More Gilt-Edged Bonds* (New York: The Macmillan Company, 1965 and London: Jonathan Cape Ltd.), p. 65. Copyright 1954, Gildrose Productions Ltd., used by permission.

First Reader: "Blessed are the meek, for they shall inherit the earth. Blessed are the peacemakers, for they shall be called sons of God."

Second Reader: "Bond whipped the gun down hard on the back of the wooly skull. . . . A final short scream was driven out of the man as he sailed down the few feet to the stairs. His head hit the side of the iron bannisters. . . . There was a short crash as he caromed off some obstacle, then a pause, then a mingled thud and crack as he hit the ground." [9]

First Reader: "And suddenly there was with the angel a multitude of the heavenly host praising God and saying, 'Glory to God in the highest and on earth, peace among men.' "

A sudden switch from biblical to contemporary characters is effected in "You are the Man!" which may be found in the anthology. In this dialogue, David and Nathan imaginatively re-enact and enlarge David's encounter with the prophet after the Bathsheba incident. At mid-sermon, the two speakers move into the contemporary situation to discuss what happened to David and Nathan from the viewpoint of the "new morality." The sermon concludes with the reading of Psalm 51, David's confession of sin, and the announcement of God's forgiveness which is available in our own day.

"Stream of consciousness" might accurately describe a Christmas sermon preached by Pastors Robert Raines and Theodore Loder of the First Methodist Church of Germantown, Philadelphia, Pennsylvania. In this one, Mr. Raines preached a traditional Christmas sermon which was interrupted every so often by Mr. Loder, who reflected aloud the reactions and random thoughts of a typically secularized but sensitive member of the congregation. Thus it is conceivable that Mr. Raines' part could stand by itself as an Advent sermon, but it is enriched by the musings of a layman who represents the listeners' best and worst selves — selves in authentic dialogue with the preacher. The preacher does not respond directly to the layman, however, because he doesn't actually hear his thoughts. There is no feedback on the preacher's part, and so it is not dialogue in that sense.

At the morning service of the Stafford Springs United Church of Christ, Connecticut, the New Testament reading was following by the playing over the public address system of "Nowhere Man," a record by the Beatles. Glenn Wolczak and Robert

[9] *Ibid.*, pp. 69-70.

Heavilin then came into the pulpit for the sermon, with Mr. Heavilin explaining that worshipers need to be open to truth, however it may come. Mr. Wolczak then presented an "exegesis" of the song, pointing out that there is a bit of "nowhere" in each of us: a drifting, purposeless, aimless kind of living. To conclude the dialogue, Mr. Heavilin proposed a Christian response:

> I proclaim that the Christian faith is the helping hand that provides the perspective . . . the point of view . . . and demands that involvement in life which will transform a "nowhere man" into a "somewhere man," aware of life . . . Jesus as the Christ is the model for my life . . . My direction lies in serving Him and His people . . . all my neighbors and brothers.

One final sermon in the composite category is noted, however, which did involve interaction within the total congregation. The Rev. Robert E. Overstreet, pastor of the First Baptist Church of Westwood, Massachusetts, preached on *Man of La Mancha*. He sketched out the background of this Broadway musical based on the legend of Don Quixote, interspersing stereophonic recordings from its music, and made the music itself the other partner in a chancel dialogue in which he attempted to respond to the meanings in the lyrics. With considerable skill and insight, Mr. Overstreet thus had dialogue with the text of the musical, and then involved his audience in further exploration of its implications.

The increasingly popular device of involving laymen in dialogue with each other following the service of worship has not been discussed, for it does not fall within our definition of dialogue preaching as a function within worship.

The descriptions in the "composite" category represent only a few of the novel, creative dialogues which are being presented in churches of nearly every denomination, youth gatherings, chapel services, ecumenical conferences, and in homes.

Both the standard and the experimental forms of dialogue preaching augur well for the future of the pulpit ministry. The extent to which the dialogical form will be employed in the next few years is unknown; the value to be derived can only be guessed at. The enthusiastic response of both clergymen and laymen to dialogue sermons is convincing evidence, however, that dialogue preaching has come into the church's life to stay; and that it will increasingly enrich and extend the message of the gospel to a disturbed and bleeding world.

4

THE VALUES
OF DIALOGUE PREACHING

WHETHER PREACHERS have used the dialogue method or not, they generally have an opinion about it. The fact that only a minority of the clergy have ever participated in dialogue preaching might suggest that they are opposed to the idea. Actually, it is quite probable that most ministers have never seriously considered the possibility; a considerable number responded to the questionnaire study by saying that they had not thought about doing dialogues. A number of other reasons were also given, however, which need to be faced by persons who do think about the possibility of preaching in dialogue.

RESERVATIONS ABOUT DIALOGUE PREACHING

Many of the respondents answered that they simply felt unable to break out of the traditional preaching pattern. Some frankly admitted being bound by tradition; some said they lacked the courage to try something novel. Others confessed a fear that they would receive negative criticism from their congregations. Certainly the clergyman who is healthy enough to admit such fears is healthy enough to evaluate them frankly. Perhaps some of these men will now find the courage to become more adventuresome in their homiletical approach.

Another area of difficulty expressed by our respondents is that of finding suitable partners. The senior minister of a large church can assign an assistant pastor to aid him, but the pastor working alone does not have this option. We have seen that dialogue preaching does not always require another clergyman, however; occasionally even one person can do it by assuming two roles. In addition, in every parish there are informed, articulate laymen, young and old, who might enjoy such an experience if they were encouraged by their pastor to take part.

Some men feel that preaching in dialogue requires skills which they lack: a lively imagination, the dramatic sense, an ability to write crisp dialogue, acting know-how. While such skills are valuable, no one really expects the dialogue preacher to be an actor. Indeed, to make the occasion of a dialogue sermon into a heavy theatrical performance could deny the integrity of a person's ministry. God can speak his word through drama, and frequently does, but an effective preacher need not choose one of the more highly dramatic motifs of dialogue preaching. He can use the skills he has in a format which differs only slightly from his usual way of working.

It is natural to hesitate about a radical departure from the ordinary. The minister in a hospital chaplaincy or a night minister in a metropolitan theatre district might well hesitate to preach in any form; some who are in such specialized ministries responded in this manner. More to the point, however, are the replies of those who have what they feel to be significant objections to dialogue preaching as a method of communicating the gospel.

Objectors to dialogue preaching propose a wide variety of reasons for rejecting it or hoisting warnings about it. Some of these are very thoughtful and have real validity; others are easily countered.

One objection, for example, is that not all sermon themes lend themselves to dialogue preaching. True!

Others object that a dialogue sermon may ignore the real issues in the listeners' minds. Is that possibility not equally valid for a traditional sermon, if not more so?

Some other objections:

1. Dialogue preaching takes extensive preparation.
2. The congregation needs to be prepared for listening.[1]

---

[1] For a more complete treatment of preaching from the listener's viewpoint, see William D. Thompson, *A Listener's Guide to Preaching* (Nashville: Abingdon Press, 1966).

3. Feedback from the congregation is very important but hard to secure.

4. It is difficult to maintain unity within the sermon.

5. Achieving a satisfactory resolution of the issue is also difficult.

It may be true that one or another of these objections applies to dialogical preaching in a different degree than to monological preaching. For example, pastors raise issues that cluster around the reactions of the congregation to dialogue preaching. Chancel dialogue, they say, poses several serious problems. People may tend to look at it as play-acting — as a show, unreal, contrived, and phony. Also, it may startle traditionalists by its novelty, causing them to be caught up in the method rather than to relate to the message. Still another objection is that the audience may be left out entirely while the participants battle out an issue which is of interest only to them.

These problems definitely occur at times. People are startled by having a fellow parishioner stand up during the sermon introduction to voice his disagreement with the pastor. Persons who are slow to accept change may not easily adapt to the idea of hearing two voices from the pulpit. Worshipers whose need is to hear a word from the living God may indeed feel frozen out of a chancel debate on a question which does not seem to merit being asked. Whose fault is it when a dialogue sermon goes astray or misses the mark? The answer is that either the speakers or the audience may be to blame. If the speakers are dealing with unimportant questions, or with matters whose importance they have failed to communicate, if they use language which people cannot readily understand, ramble off into insignificant bypaths, fail to articulate or speak loudly enough, they are certainly to blame. On the other hand, persons in the congregation who steel themselves against anything new can impede the effectiveness of a dialogue sermon as surely as they can stop the building of the church's educational wing. The seed which falls along the path or on rocky ground is not to be blamed if it does not take root and grow; the condition of the soil is crucial.

The sermon which involves the congregation in direct verbal dialogue as an intrinsic part of the sermonic presentation poses some difficult problems. Clergymen who have used this method warn about three primary dangers: (1) initiating the discussion, especially in a large congregation, is very difficult; (2) some persons tend to dominate any discussion, and will dominate it even in the sanctuary; (3) the minister may pose as an answer-box and cut off honest dialogue with the people. The minister who is highly skilled in discussion leadership will be able to surmount these barriers.

In short, the objections raised to dialogue preaching have a great deal more to do with the sensitivity of the persons handling it than with any inherent defects in the method.

ADVANTAGES OF DIALOGUE PREACHING

Persons who have done dialogue preaching are almost unanimous in their contention that it produces a higher interest level on the part of the congregation. One would expect this to be true, just as one finds that a moving window display will attract more attention than a still one. The mere fact of having vocal variety and contrast between voices will attract and hold attention, at least initially.

There is a great deal more than this, however, to account for the heightened audience interest. Dialogue preaching gets people involved in the communication of ideas. Whether the two persons are debating a contemporary issue from the pulpit or the pastor is fielding questions from the congregation following the initial presentation, the listeners are inevitably drawn into the process. The auditors tend to identify with the speakers and points of view being expressed, and this intellectual (if not physical) involvement is a second prime value of dialogue preaching which, we find, is less likely to occur with the standard, traditional sermon.

A third advantage of dialogue preaching over the monological style is the opportunity it affords for sharpening issues. The traditional sermon can, of course, present issues clearly; the best sermons do. Dialogue preaching *must* sharpen the issues, for it is the nature of the method to keep raising and dealing with the questions dictated by a common search for truth. When the congregation is given the opportunity to ask questions of the minister, some perceptive person almost invariably challenges an assumption held by him but not by all of his congregation. Or a listener who has not understood a theological term may ask about its meaning, speaking for other listeners who have previously gone away bewildered and confused. When two speakers present the sermon from the chancel, one of them will probably take the responsibility for making sure the subject is understood, the words are defined, the abstract ideas are made concrete, and the right questions are raised. This will certainly happen in a sermon of inquiry, and probably in many of the other types as well.

Still another advantage of dialogue preaching is that it frequently forces listeners to consider ideas which they might otherwise have blocked out of their minds. Studies in listening show that people tend to tune out the ideas which challenge their own belief structure. (Some call this the phenomenon of "cognitive dissonance.") The person who hears his pastor hold forth on fair housing legislation, for example, may well switch to another channel mentally if he is unsympathetic to the idea. But when the argument is proposed by a fellow member in the next pew he will listen, at least, if only because of the novelty of the situation.

Allied with this reason for doing dialogue preaching is the tendency of the method to deal with the real questions and tensions that people have. The traditional preacher never intends to ignore the problem areas of his parishioners' lives, but he frequently misses the mark by a wide margin. Given a chance, laymen are delighted to help their pastor tackle the questions which really bother them. Fellow ministers may use the opportunity for dialogue to handle a subject they would not ordinarily treat when preaching alone. Because he may be viewed as one who is playing a role, a minister may introduce advanced ideas he feels his parish is not quite ready to accept; he has planted the seed thought without threatening anyone.

The final advantage to be considered lies in the broadening effect of dialogue on both preacher and people. The preacher who attempts a dialogue sermon casts his lot with the progressive Christians who are using the latest methods in the communication of the gospel. He may not qualify for the *avant garde* of clergy — and probably doesn't want to — but he acknowledges by his choice of a communication medium that he is in step with a fast-paced, seeking, open-minded age. The laymen who participate in dialogue preaching discover that religious truth is not a dry non-discussible subject fit only for trained theologians, but a lively, life-centered, exciting area of exploration which can challenge the best thinking they can bring to it.

THE DELIVERY FACTOR

Of course, any of these advantages may be lost if the sermon is ineptly presented. How can the dialogue preacher be certain that his carefully prepared material really gets across to people?

The dialogue preacher has the same options for delivery which are open to the traditional preacher: speaking from manuscript, from notes or an outline, or full memorization. Most of the weaknesses of dialogue preaching which relate to the delivery factor probably arise out of the pastor's using an unfamiliar method. One may be tempted, for example, to write down every word and give a chancel dialogue from full manuscript; it is a unique experience and therefore ought to be carefully prepared. The value of a well written manuscript is beyond dispute. What may go wrong is that the sermon will sound pedantic, artificial, or unreal if the preacher is not accustomed to reading a manuscript aloud. If a manuscript is to be used, it should be read with a high degree of skill and freedom in order to achieve the spontaneity which characterizes the best preaching.

The memorization of material is both time-consuming and dangerous. Particularly in the give-and-take of dialogue preaching, memorization is questionable. If a preacher ordinarily memorizes a manuscript, he may feel comfortable handling the first part of congregational discussion — his own introduction — in this way. There is little possibility of the participants in chancel dialogue using the memorization approach with good effect.

The use of an outline is probably the most promising method of delivery for dialogue preaching. The outline may be highly detailed and spread out before each participant on his lectern. It may, on the other hand, be a simple listing of topics to be covered. It may be somewhere between — a modest outline of ideas, perhaps with supporting illustrations suggested by a word or two. Using an outline gives some order and form to the presentation without making it the sterile, lifeless thing a manuscript often produces.

Certainly the method of presentation to which the preacher is accustomed is the method with which to begin. One may find that the requirements of dialogue preaching are so different, a new set of techniques is needed. However, this will seldom be the case.

Another factor which must be considered is the mental agility of the participants. The Rev. John Huess, rector of Trinity Church (Episcopal) in New York City wrote us in a letter:

> If a dialogue sermon is to be really effective, it cannot be prepared for and written down in the normal fashion. The persons who engage in a dialogue must be people who have the sharpness of mind to speak with authority and mostly off-the-cuff. . . . [This means] that it has to be spontaneous. When I work with Joseph McCulloch, we sit down for about an hour before the dialogue and simply talk to each other as we would in ordinary conversation about the general theme which we want to discuss. This warm-up is very important.

There is no one "right way" to prepare or present a dialogue sermon. What is necessary is that it sound spontaneous, real, human, authentic, conversational. Without experience, most of us need to do some experimenting. We need to hear and heed the reactions of those who hear us. We need, through the tape recorder, to hear ourselves. Above all, we need to develop willingness to try new methods and a sensitivity which will enable us to evaluate our experiments accurately.

THE CHALLENGE OF DIALOGUE

You can do dialogue preaching! More and more clergymen are doing it and reporting their results enthusiastically. Laymen of all faiths who have listened to dialogue preaching and participated in it believe that its potential is tremendous. No one expects it to replace traditional, one-man preaching. If you use it as an integral part of your year's preaching effort, you should experience at first hand what the Rev. Vern Campbell of Milan, Michigan, wrote us:

> As long as there is give and take between two or more people in front of an audience, that audience is going to listen!

. . . and what the Rev. Edward T. Clark of St. Louis, Missouri, wrote:

> People become involved at the level of their concern and need—the minister is forced to listen and become involved beyond his own concerns and ideas.

. . . and what the Rev. Bruce Campbell of Richmond, Virginia, said:

[Dialogue preaching provides] the opportunity to say things in a vitally new way, unexpected and therefore possibly heard in a way never before possible.

Monological preaching has dominated the church's communicative effort for centuries; it has done its work well. As an exclusive method, however, it tends to limit, sometimes even distort, the Christian message. Its content may communicate the gospel accurately and movingly, but its method cannot help but emphasize the authority of God, the revelatory nature of his Word, and the passivity of man. Dialogue preaching, by its very nature, communicates the "other side of God." It says that God is in encounter with his people, that he is listening as well as talking. In addition, it involves and demands a personal participation on the part of each individual. It makes people react and respond to the divine Word and to each other, actively and creatively, enabling them to move toward those relationships of love which are man's highest response to the love of the Lord.

The person who listens creatively to a chancel dialogue or who participates vocally in a congregational dialogue may learn some unique insights about the Christian faith; he may find that some of those dry-as-dust theological terms actually have a relation to his own experience at home, in the office or shop, at school or at city hall; he may discover through dialogue a moment of spiritual ecstasy or sheer joy in the engagement of meaningful ideas. Whatever happens, he will find himself responding in some way to the Word and will of God. The nature of that response is up to him and the Holy Spirit; the inevitability of his responding is assured by the force of the dialogue form, which God may well have meant for such a time as this.

5

AN ANTHOLOGY
OF DIALOGUE SERMONS

THIS ANTHOLOGY consists of dialogue sermons actually preached. Unfortunately, these are exclusively what we have termed *chancel* dialogue; since we have no knowledge of any *congregational* dialogues being recorded, we are unable to furnish the reader with an actual transcript of such a discussion.

This sampling of fine chancel dialogues illustrates the general types described in chapter three. "If I Should Die," "The Many Masks of Christians," and "The Unity We Seek" exemplify the dialogue of *support;* "No Further Trek" illustrates the dialogue of *inquiry;* "Preacher Meets Hippie," "Ins and Outs," and "Don't Blame God" represent the dialogue of *conflict.* "Don't Blame God" is also an example of the *multilogue* or dialogue involving more than two voices. "You Are the Man!" is one of many unorthodox styles of dialogue we have chosen to call *composite.*

The reader will notice a contrast in style and language as well as in the function of the participants. "If I Should Die," for example, is written in long, extended speeches, while "The Many Masks of Christians" seems to be a crisp, choppy vernacular. While in general the latter style is preferred because it more nearly represents the shorter speeches and quick give-and-take of real conversation, obviously the style the dialogist uses will reflect his purpose, subject, and occasion. A pastor-student dialogue such as "The Many Masks of Christians" would naturally find expression in the modern idiom and the natural spontaneity of modern youth. A more philosophical discussion or a topic that calls for a great deal of technical or historical information, such as that provided by the participants in the interfaith dialogue "The Unity We Seek," may require long paragraphs without many breaks or changes. In the dialogue of conflict, however, such a style, no matter how erudite, would generally seem verbose. The clash of personalities requires quick, lively exchanges like the exclamations, rejoinders, rapid comments and breaks of actual speech when there are disagreements and outbursts. The preacher and the hippie in our fifth sermon could not possibly use stylish sentences, pedantic language, or long, heavy speeches without producing a dud. The "Ins and Outs," on the other hand, is a different kind of conflict. Since it is not a direct clash between two characters at a given point in time but rather a reflective discourse involving the representatives of two camps speaking for their respective constituents, the authors did not find it necessary to make the exchange a terse repartee of the order of "Preacher Meets Hippie." In our final illustration, "You Are the Man!" the contrast in language and phrasing between the initial biblical dialogue and the later contemporary discussion of modern sex morality shows how the dialogue preacher may tailor his style according to the content — time, context, characterizations, etc.

Some background information pertaining to the circumstances of its original presentation, and the manner in which the dialogue was prepared is included with each of the sermons in the anthology as a means of helping those who are still uncertain as to how a dialogue sermon actually materializes.

Finally, let us take this opportunity to thank those who created and presented the dialogues included in this anthology. We appreciate both their creative efforts and their permissions for us to include their works in this volume. Pioneers all, they represent that growing class of modern preachers who are the pulpit innovators of today and the homiletical heroes of tomorrow.

DIALOGUE OF SUPPORT:
"IF I SHOULD DIE"

THE REV. RALPH LIGHTBODY, minister of the Drexel Hill Baptist Church, Drexel Hill, Pennsylvania, had come to believe that the traditional practices surrounding the death and burial of church members were generally less than Christian. Knowing that there was a great deal of popular interest in the subject provoked by Waugh's *The Loved One* and Mitford's *The American Way of Death*, and since many persons responded favorably to his suggestions for change made in the context of preparing for funerals, he decided that the time was ripe for a formal presentation.

He wanted to achieve some measurable change in the funeral practices of the church, an ambitious objective for any sermon. He also wanted to provide an adequate biblical and theological basis for this change. Finally, he wanted to couch the presentation in as attractive and compelling a way as possible.

The method he chose was a dialogue sermon with a member of his congregation who teaches preaching at the Eastern Baptist Theological Seminary in nearby Philadelphia, the Rev. William Thompson. The approach was to raise and answer a series of questions with which the congregation could identify.

The introduction claims the attention of the congregation by asserting that the subject of death has been neglected and misplaced; it sets up a tension immediately which demands resolution. It then raises the thought, "In the light of my faith, what shall I do?" A series of questions follows: What are the influences which provoke our interest in the subject? What does the Bible have to say about it? What should be the church's role in the chain reaction of experiences that death initiates? How are we to express our grief? What are some things a Christian should do in dealing with death?

The preachers evidently anticipated correctly the questions people were really asking; the dialogue sermon was the main topic of discussion for weeks following its presentation. Better yet is Mr. Lightbody's report that the sermon marked a turning point in the congregation's practice of handling funerals; increasing numbers of church members, encouraged by the experience of taking "a fresh look at the end of life," chose to hold a private burial service for family and close friends, followed a few days later by a memorial service in the church sanctuary. Equally important was the ease with which persons approached the subject in conversation, knowing that their pastor was sympathetic to their feelings, and eager to help them through the experience in either a traditional or unique way.

"IF I SHOULD DIE"

Ralph H. Lightbody and William D. Thompson

Lightbody: We are all familiar with the ancient and traditional lament of the manager of a sports team whose men had just lost a close and exciting game: "We wuz robbed!" In a sense, the same kind of lament is justified in connection with the subject that is to be the center of our concern this morning. We have been robbed! The province of death has been moved outside the framework in which it rightfully should be placed.

It has been moved outside the framework of normal conversation and discussion. This most universal of all experiences, that of concern and deep consideration through all our lives as we face the fact and reality of death, is a subject we think about as seldom as possible, and discuss with great hesitancy. That which we cannot avoid in fact becomes the subject we seek to avoid in every way possible until, in the inevitability of life's pattern, we are thrust against death and have to face it and deal with it.

It has been moved outside the framework of

Christian faith. That which we do when death comes to a loved one, the traditions we carry out, the customs we follow, are much more the result of our response to the culture of our day and its demands upon us than they are the claims of Christian faith. "What will *they* think?" — "they" being our relatives and friends, our business associates, our society — is the question that shapes our decisions and actions at the time of death with far greater frequency than the question: "In the light of my faith, what shall I do?"

It has been moved outside the framework of the church. We bring our children to the church for dedication. We make our professions of faith in the church. We come to the church for the beginning of the experience we call marriage. But so often, in our day, the church is bypassed in connection with the very experience that so desperately needs the illumination that the church offers through the gospel it proclaims.

Because we have been robbed, both as Christians and as a Christian church, I believe we are justified in taking time to consider, in the setting of Christian worship, the subject of death and funeral practices. If we fail to do this, we are assenting to the robbery by our silence, and have no reason to complain.

Thompson: Complaining about the funeral business is becoming one of America's great indoor pastimes. It isn't only the church that is raising questions about funeral practices; it is society in general. The questions are naturally generating other questions — in the minds and offices of funeral directors, florists, cemetery people, and those of a dozen other industries that depend for their livelihood on perpetuating or extending current funeral practices.

Lightbody: There are some interesting books that have stirred up the country about funerals, aren't there?

Thompson: Yes, one is called *The High Cost of Dying*, and the other is *The American Way of Death*. They've

become best sellers, largely because they concen-
trate on the fantastic amount of money Americans
spend on the process of burying their dead. According to one of the authors, the average total cost of
an adult's funeral is $1,450.

Lightbody: All the facts and accusations made in these books
serve a very useful purpose, whether we agree with
them or not. They make us think, and it is my
hope that the storm they have created may cause
us all to ask, not just questions about "The American Way of Death" or about "The High Cost of
Dying," but serious and probing questions about
"The Christian Way of Death."

We need to come to some clear understanding
about our Christian convictions about death and
eternal life and to let them shape and form our
attitudes and actions. In the light of our faith, how
do we best honor the memory of a loved one?
What does our faith say about the importance of
the body — before death and after death? How are
we to let go of our grief and sorrow? How are we
to pick up and go on? Does the faith we profess
speak to these questions? We need to do more than
just criticize costs and condemn customs which
may offend. Don't we need to examine all of this
in the light of faith? In the light of the teachings
of the Bible?

Thompson: Someone has said that the Bible is a matter of life
and death. It has a great deal more to say about
life than death, however; and what it does tell us
about death and existence in the hereafter is not
always clear. The writer of Ecclesiastes — probably
Solomon — presents death as the absolute end of
existence. He says there is no life beyond the grave.
Yet Jesus told, in vivid detail, a story about the
experiences of someone who had died. John wrote,
in Revelation, about the ultimate destiny of men,
but in strange imagery. The notions many people
have of the life hereafter — especially of hell, with
its forked-tail Devil and burning waters — come

from Dante's *Inferno* or the imagination of some preacher, and not from the Bible. The Bible's teaching about hell focuses on the awfulness of eternal separation from God.

One idea that does emerge clearly from the Bible, however, is the temporary character of life. The Bible suggests that life is a *pilgrimage* — a brief time spent by the human soul on the earth; as one poet has put it, a "prelude to eternity." The Apostle Paul, in his Second Letter to the Corinthians, likened the human body to a tent. He said that death is a release from this most unsatisfactory thing in which we live. He said that death enables the believer in Christ to live in a "building from God, a house not made with hands; eternal in the heavens." The writer of Psalm 90 looked at life as a blade of grass. "In the morning it flourishes and is renewed; in the evening it fades and withers." The apostle James wrote to the early church: "What is your life? For you are a mist that appears for a little time and then vanishes."

But another idea, that goes along with the temporariness of life, is the supreme worth of human life. It was in the Sermon on the Mount that Jesus placed human life over against every other form of life. Of the birds of the air, Jesus asked: "Are you not of more value than they?" Indeed, the witness of the New Testament is that we human beings are so worthwhile that God gave his Son to die for us.

Lightbody: If we are right in taking time to ask, "What does the Bible say about death?" we also have reason to ask another question that may help us to arrive at a more satisfying understanding of the whole subject: "What should the role of the church be in the chain reaction of experiences that death sets off?" If I am to answer this question, I must confess that I do so with some firm convictions. I am a jealous minister at this point — jealous of anything that seeks to occupy the place that the church — with its affirmations about hope and promise and eternal life — ought rightfully to have when death visits its fellowship.

An atheist has a perfect right to any combination of the sentimental and the secular that may please or ease or even blur the experience of death, but a Christian, a member of a church, ought to seek to carry out, even in his style of dying, the claim of the church — expressed so clearly in our church covenant when it speaks of the church as deserving "a sense of sacred preeminence over all institutions of human origin." If there were only one plea that I could make, it would be to hold the funeral service of every church member in the church — and nowhere else. I have hinted at the reasons for this. A church funeral or memorial service allows death to be faced, dealt with, and confronted in a natural setting, in a setting where many experiences, some joyous and some solemn, take place. We are not dealing with a building dedicated to death alone, but one set apart for bringing God's meaning into all of life's experiences, into the totality of human existence. May I urge you to discuss this in your homes and make this request of your loved ones that there may be no hesitancy about this decision when death visits your family circle. From my experience, I could share many testimonies of families who, having made this choice, found cause to rejoice in it.

Let me raise another broad subject that we ought to consider in this setting and discuss in the conversations that we hope you will carry on after this one is concluded. The question is one that turns our attention to those who are left after death has broken into the family circle. "What are our needs in such a situation?" We often hear the statement: "The funeral is for the living." What are the deep human needs that should be met?

Thompson: One that comes to my mind is the need to express one's grief. Our American culture is rather strange at this point. It tells us that we must not express our grief openly, or that we should be very cautious about it. Men, especially, operate under this cultural taboo. Though we are theoretically as human as women, we are never supposed to cry. I remember my own tension at this point when, during college days, my father died; and last year, when my mother died. I felt real grief, and wanted to cry. And I did, but not when I needed to the most, because of the conditioning of our way of life. In the Bible, many hundreds of deaths are recorded, and no censure is ever visited upon a person for the expression of his grief. Our Lord himself found a natural, normal release of his sorrow at the death of Lazarus: "Jesus wept."

Of course, there can be an unhealthy dimension to the expression of grief. Some people give way to uncontrolled crying. We say that they "go to pieces." Others enter upon a prolonged or permanent period of mourning. They never really face the change that death has brought and never return to as normal a life as is possible.

A more subtle way of distorting the expression of grief is in the spending of unreasonable amounts of money for the funeral service. Without blaming the commercial interests for this, we nevertheless must face the conclusions of specialists in human personality who tell us that we all have guilt feelings about the person who has died. We may recall some unkind word or act. We may be totally unaware of any specific wrong we have done, but merely feel that the funeral is our last chance to "do something nice" for Mother or Grandpa or Uncle Ed. We do not even face the reality that Uncle Ed is in no position to care.

But there are healthy ways to express one's grief. There is crying. There is the honest facing of one's guilt feelings, or one's uneasiness, however undefined. To talk freely and in confidence with one's minister at the coming of death is one of the best things you can do. There is a normal life to be returned to, as quickly as possible.

Lightbody: I wonder if some of the excesses of expressing grief and remorse don't center upon the body of the departed?

Thompson: Yes, I think so. Do you feel that seeing the body of the deceased is one of the needs to be met?

Lightbody: When we get to the question of the display and final disposition of the body of a loved one, we are entering into an area of sharp controversy. Some would insist that, in terms of meeting the need of facing the reality of death, some display of the body is essential. There are others who maintain, just as vehemently, that the presence of the body after death only interferes with the recognition of reality following death. Perhaps a private committal service should be held for members of the immediate family, and then, in a day or two, a memorial service. Certainly the viewing of the body is one subject that should be considered seriously and discussed by a family before death occurs, so that wishes may be carefully honored.

There is an increasing unanimity of opinion among Christians, and a growing concern, that the public display of the body after death does little to honor the deceased, or to give comfort to the survivors, and detracts from the religious affirmation that would stress the continuity of life. The ancient Egyptians gave much attention to the preparation and glorification of the body, but they had a reason, in the light of their religious teachings. They believed that, if the body were attractive enough, the soul would be coaxed into returning to it. We have no such conviction, and thus the display of the body serves little purpose.

Now this is an area where custom seems to come into conflict with faith. We need to be strong enough in our faith — and united enough in the fellowship of the church — to shape some new patterns and develop some new traditions.

There is almost unanimous opinion among churchmen that, at the time of a funeral service or a memorial service, the casket should remain closed, regardless of what the pattern may have previously been.

Two further words about the body.

There is a growing tendency to make provision for the donation of the eyes to an eye-bank or the body to a medical school. This kind of decision also needs to be made in quiet and reflective days when one's wishes can be clearly known.

Again, arrangements should be made, well in advance, concerning the final disposition of the body, whether by burial or cremation, and where the remains are to be placed. The subject of cremation versus the more normal pattern of burial could well be the subject of another discussion. The main point is this: in regard to all that may be said about the body, our decisions and practices ought to underscore the truth of Luther's words: "The body they may kill; God's truth abideth still." Our present practices and customs do not always do this.

Let us go on to another matter. How are we to express our grief and give vent to our sorrow? Surely, to stand without emotion is not normal. What does the Christian faith say to this? What is the right way to help someone in sorrow?

Thompson: A contemporary specialist in pastoral counseling says that the pastor does some of his most important work when he is saying nothing. This is startling news to some ministers!

Along with "healing" and "guiding," he uses the word "sustaining" to describe a significant function of the minister, especially in the time of death. By "sustaining," he means "standing by" — being there — to communicate without words whatever strength or reassurance one can bring, building largely upon the confidence of past associations. A predecessor of mine in a Chicago pastorate excelled at this. So good was his pastoral work, so close his relationships to his people, that he could transform the mood of a grieving family by entering the room. But sustaining is something we can all do.

Far better than the stilted phrases of sympathy I have heard so often in the many deaths that have come to our rather large immediate family is the mere presence of those who have shared in the giving and receiving of love. So, too, is the action of friends and neighbors who bring in casseroles and provide beds for out-of-town relatives, record the flowers and cards that come and do the many, many unusual jobs from which the family needs relief.

All of this leads to what is probably the final question: how, then, does a Christian deal with death when it comes?

Lightbody: If you want me to suggest a particular and specific answer and pattern, we need to remember at least two things: first, each situation may shape its own answer; and, secondly, any suggestions such as I am going to make are subjective. They grow out of my experience in conducting over 330 funerals in the last fifteen years. They grow out of my personal feelings and faith. These are my answers. You will need to work out your own.

First, I would suggest that immediately, at the time of the death of a loved one, you should call your pastor.

Then, shortly after the death of a loved one, I believe it would be most fitting to hold a private service of committal, preferably at the graveside, where the Scriptures are read, prayers offered, and the body laid to rest.

Plans should then be made for a suitable memorial service to be held whenever possible in the sanctuary or chapel of the church. Such a service should capture the notes of affirmation of faith and gratitude for the life shared with us. The particular qualities of contributions of the deceased will shape the selection of Scriptures and poetry and hymns. The service should pay tribute to the life that has been lived and commit that life into the fullness of God's love and the brightness of eternity. Hope, not gloom, should be the note that is struck. If some way can be devised through memorial designations, in place of an overly elaborate display of flowers, to express the concern that an individual has had during his lifetime for his church or for some particular project, this will add meaning to the funeral experience.

Before and after such a memorial service, times should be set aside for the visiting of members of the immediate family. A room in the church could well serve such a purpose. A funeral home can also be used for this experience. We need to express, through our Christian fellowship, our support of each other in times of tragedy and distress and to strengthen our common faith that "God will not leave us or forsake us" and "nothing can separate us from the love of Christ."

Keeping in mind the double need of remembering with simplicity the love of one who has died and of affirming our faith in the love that never dies will help us to make of the events that follow the death of a loved one not so much a sign of resignation as an affirmation of faith.

Thompson: "If I Should Die" is the title of this sermon. We know the setting of the phrase. It comes from a prayer that many of us learned as children. But we also know that, for us, the *if* doesn't belong. We know that we shall all die — some of us, perhaps, within the next few months. Even to say this disturbs us, because we do not like to talk or think about death or funerals — especially our own. But we are a people who have named Christ as Lord of all — of all aspects of life and of its end, which is death. As we must, we seek his will for death and for all that goes with it.

From the Bible and the tradition of the church,

we have learned something about life and death. From our own experience of the pain of death and the grief of the funeral, we have formed some opinions of our own. In the issues we have tried to face this morning, we have raised some further questions and given some tentative answers. Our purpose is not to attack the funeral business or to upset the traditions of the community. It is rather to ask you to take a fresh look at the end of life — yours and of those near you — and to bring your attitudes and your practice into conformity with the will of God as your church and the Holy Spirit help you to understand it.

I trust that all of us can make the determination of the apostle Paul our own. He said: "It is my eager expectation and hope . . . that with full courage now as always Christ will be honored in my body, whether by life or by death" (Philippians 1:20).

DIALOGUE OF SUPPORT:
"THE MANY MASKS OF CHRISTIANS"

THE CHURCH OF THE BRETHREN in Lancaster, Pennsylvania, was the scene of this lively dialogue sermon preached by Theodore E. Whitacre, associate pastor, and David Martin, a college student, on October 30, 1966. It was delivered to a congregation of 500 persons of varied socio-economic backgrounds, and it was apparently well received. Mr. Whitacre emphasizes the need of careful preparation and repeated practice in order to achieve the desired effect. He describes the sermon as a joint effort involving at least thirty hours of preparation:

> He wrote and so did I. Then we got together. We tape recorded our conversation. We went back and wrote separately, then back together again at a typewriter. We typed out our dialogue. Then we polished it for phrasing, paragraphing, etc. Then we practiced a couple of hours in the sanctuary, Dave in the pulpit, I at the lectern.

The dialogue has a crisp, vernacular style which would give it the sound of spontaneity and relevancy. Its conversational quality is a product of language and style; the short speeches and fast give-and-take require an audience to stay awake and stay involved. Note also that the sermon builds to a conclusion that is underscored and enhanced by the joining of both voices in two key lines at the close of the dialogue. It would be difficult for anyone to miss the point with this strong vocal emphasis at the close!

"THE MANY MASKS OF CHRISTIANS"

Theodore E. Whitacre and David Martin

Ted: A mask is for covering the face.

Dave: It is used for disguise.

Ted: Masks have dramatic, festive, and religious uses.

Dave: Tomorrow night is the one night of the year when one can dress in whatever style he pleases. . . .

Ted: And still be accepted in society. Whether it be the costume of Daisy Mae in Li'l Abner, or a clown.

Dave: But though we have said that this is the only day we can wear a mask and still be accepted by society, is it not true that we wear masks all the time?

Ted: I think I know what you mean.

Dave: Well, to me, a mask is basically a false front. It is a facade we use to hide our real selves.

Ted: You mean that the real self is the mask behind all masks?

Dave: No. The real self is not a mask at all. The real self is that which we are, how we feel at any given time. To hide what we really are — and to create a false image — is a barrier to personal relationships.

Ted: I agree. But are there not times when we need to protect the true self by using a mask?

Dave: I would think of it not in terms of protecting the true self but in protecting others from the faults of that true self.

Ted: I've lost you, now. Can you clarify?

Dave: Take the instance where two friends agree to meet at a
         certain place at a given time. One of them is late — the
         other has obligations to meet. When the latecomer ar-
         rives, his friend is annoyed — but, should not express his
         disappointment in too overt a manner.

Ted: You mean he should complain just a little bit.

Dave: It depends on the nature of the relationship. A mask
         must be appropriate to the situation.

Ted: Oh, you mean that there lies on the table a variety of
         masks from which one can choose just as there is a wide
         selection of false faces in stores at Halloween. And one
         should wear the mask which meets the situation.

Dave: "Should wear the mask which meets the situation?" —
         well, to me, the Christian way to approach the problem
         is one of true forgiveness.

Ted: So, if I am the one waiting for my friend who is late
         then I should say as soon as he arrives, "That's all right.
         Don't mention it. You're forgiven."

Dave: Sorry about that —

Ted: Is this the true self speaking?

Dave: Well, one should not create a facade.

Ted: Here's a question then . . . Should a Christian ever be
         seen wearing the face of impatience or anger? Should
         this be part of the real self's daily apparel?

Dave: You have posed a problem. On the one hand we must be
         kind, but on the other we need to be true to our own
         feelings.

Ted: It is a dilemma. Have we not been taught that a Chris-
         tian should wear the mask of kindness? No, not the *mask*
         of kindness but *to be* kind. Does impatience or anger
         ever have a place within the context of kindness?

Dave: Not kindness, but love.

Ted: You mean a Christian can be angry but still love?

Dave: Of course. Anger directed at the person's deeds rather
         than the person — at his attitudes rather than his being.

Ted: How can you be angry at a person's deeds or attitudes?
         I think that's impossible.

Dave: That's right — you cannot separate actions and thoughts
         from the person.

Ted: So — what are you trying to say?

Dave: You simply cannot let anger dominate love.

Ted: Do the masks of anger and love ever find themselves in conflict?

Dave: Yes, at times. But anger is a Christian response. Anger at prejudice. Anger at discrimination. At whatever is unloving. We find that we must frequently shield others from the effects of unrestrained anger. "Control yourself," is the slogan used by Madison Avenue to signal the beginning of a mask. Thus masks can be used, and rightfully so, to communicate with others so that people are not repulsed by the expressions of our feelings.

Ted: Does this not differ from what you said earlier when you said that a false face is a barrier to communication?

Dave: Yes, I can see that it does. We did agree earlier that a mask can be used for communication. I think we hinted, didn't we, that it can also be a barrier to communication — so extensive that it prevents us from expressing what we really are and feel.

Ted: So — to disguise oneself can be either an asset or a liability.

Dave: More liability than asset. You know — I believe that if people, especially Christians, could achieve a good relationship with God, they would need not to worry about masks.

Ted: Now wait a minute, Dave. Who wants God to see him as he really is? We keep telling ourselves that God sees us in the dark as well as in the light. There was once a little girl who said to her mother at bedtime, after being told that she need not be afraid in the dark because God was there: "I know you're there, God, but don't you move or you'll scare me to death." We keep telling ourselves that God is omnipresent, but do you think he really is?

Dave: I guess we do not act as if we believe it.

Ted: But we have to be ourselves — and sometimes being ourselves means doing those things we can't stand to see others doing. Sometimes when we are truly ourselves we are loving, and other times —

Dave: I don't know. But I do not believe that a mature Christian is divided into several persons such as a businessman, family man, Sunday Christian and weekday playboy. These are masks, and to tell you the truth I do not like to see people wearing them.

Ted: Why not? Doesn't he have to be a business man at this moment and a member of the immediate family the next? It sounds like you think one should become all things to all men. I know that is what Paul said, but I am not sure what he meant. When he was preaching to Gentiles he would refrain from talking about Jewish customs which they might find strange, and would try to put himself in the same position as his hearers. Particularly in Athens, where dialogue was customary, Paul was careful to respect conscientious scruples which he himself did not share.

Dave: Well, let me put it another way. For one to appear as though he is something when he is not — this, to me, is alien to what I think God's will is for man.

Ted: Yes, I see what you mean . . . I really don't know. I am not always sure what the will of God is.

Dave: I'm not either, but take for instance civil rights. I think I am justified in saying that many persons wear the Sunday morning mask and say that God's children should live together, regardless of race, or color, and that God is no respecter of persons. But where is that kind, uplifted face when, during the week, a family of a different color moves in next door?

Ted: Well, there may be some white families one may not want living next door to him.

Dave: You completely missed my point. Instead of hearing what I said, you defended those I accused.

Ted: OK. You said that we should be consistent — right?

Dave: Yes. By that I mean that the principles, beliefs, and attitudes of a person remain constant with him, regardless of whether he is in church, at work, or at home.

Ted: You mean they *should* remain constant.

Dave: Yes. The conscious change of attitude according to the situation is an unchristian use of masks. What I really have in mind is the type of person who professes Christian principles on Sunday, but on Monday goes to the seventh ward to collect high rent from poverty-stricken people, beyond the value of the property they occupy.

Ted: That is deplorable, wearing the mask of a Christian while taking advantage of one's fellowman. Most of us here do not own property in the seventh ward, but are there not other instances where we wear the false faces?

Dave: I remember when we first met. It seems like a classic Halloween party.

Ted: We did wear different faces.

Dave: You came to the door of our house wearing the most attractive mask you could find.

Ted: Thank you!

Dave: I was just going to ask if that was the best you could do.

Ted: Thanks again!

Dave: Seriously, like most people who meet strangers, you expected any number of responses from me — a good host, member of your congregation, and young college student.

Ted: You had three masks right there to choose from.

Dave: Perhaps the significant part is that their use may have been aimed at impressing you.

Ted: All of us use masks to impress people. You did use all three. You were a host — a most gracious one. You did talk about your church, and as a young college student expressed yourself in terms of questions and statements about your church. I also wore a number of masks.

Dave: The masks that we chose were probably those that we thought would be acceptable.

Ted: This is true! But sooner or later masks can lead to monologue — not dialogue — in communication. We have talked about the many masks Christians wear.

Dave: But are there not masks which Christians use to shield themselves from something rather than using the mask to shield others from themselves? What I mean is, Christians mask their faith rather than masking themselves.

Ted: You are saying that the essence of Christianity is sometimes hidden by a mask.

Dave: Yes.

Ted: What would be a mask worn by Christianity?

Dave: Legalism is one.

Ted: What is that?

Dave: Well, for our purposes this morning — legalism is a code
          of deeds and observances as a means of justification, or,
          shall we say, being saved. For example — it is thought
          among many church members today that if you observe
          certain deeds and abstain from certain practices you are
          assured eternal salvation.

Ted: You know, I grew up believing that the ones who walked
          into theatres, pool rooms, and taverns were the ones who
          were going to hell; and those who didn't would go to a
          better place.

Dave: Legalism is, if I may put it this way, the concept that
          God is a statistician.

Ted: A what?

Dave: A scorekeeper. It seems that he keeps score of the game
          between good and bad deeds. There are two rules in the
          game: "Thou shalt," and "Thou shalt not." To win in
          this game you must obey the rules.

Ted: Legalism is a mask, then, because it leads one into a mis-
          conception of Christianity. It is meaningless if it is in-
          terpreted in terms of rules.

Dave: Yes. Just for the sake of an example: one rule would be
          that a woman must wear a prayer cap for love feast?

Ted: I think some interpret that as a rule for the church.
          Others try to justify it through interpretation of Scrip-
          ture or preserving unity among the brethren.

Dave: We are not directly involved in this question, but what
          is the value of wearing the prayer veil at love feast when
          it is not worn consistently at church? Some women just
          don't feel right if they aren't wearing it. Is the prayer
          veil a mask?

Ted: We have already agreed that anything which becomes a
          barrier to one's understanding of people or ideas can be
          a mask. Even the praying of the Lord's Prayer could be
          a way of hiding one's real self. We pray, "Forgive us our
          debts as we forgive our debtors."

Dave: Yes, it is rather common for the man who owes someone
          money to vilify the person who owes him.

Ted: "Forgive us our debts as we forgive our debtors." A per-
          son who prays this honestly is not wearing a mask.

Dave: Well — the mask of legalism hinders people from attain-
       ing right relationships with God. We have dealt with
       several masks and perhaps the criteria by which we
       measure their value is the motive.

Ted: If I may pick up again where we discussed God-man re-
       lationship — motive becomes very important. And per-
       haps this is what you were getting at when you men-
       tioned love.

Dave: Remember our reading 1 Corinthians 13 as part of our
       preparation for this sermon and the many faces men-
       tioned, including the one that is truly Christian?

Ted: Yes — the faces of boastfulness, conceit, intellectualism,
       selfishness, rudeness, self-confidence, uh —

Dave: Philanthropy, martyrdom, hope, faith, thrill-seeking, and
       security —

Ted: But the most honest, helpful, long-lasting, patient —

Dave: Not a scorekeeper of wrong deeds or hard and fast rule,
       but enduring, stimulating, revealing the best in man —

Ted and Dave: Is LOVE!

Dave: The real face of Christianity is LOVE!

Ted: The essence of God is LOVE!

Dave: In a word — there are —

Ted: Three things which last forever . . .

Dave and Ted: FAITH, HOPE AND LOVE — BUT THE
       MOST SIGNIFICANT OF THESE IS LOVE.

DIALOGUE OF SUPPORT:
"THE UNITY WE SEEK"

ECUMENISM IS PERHAPS the most striking religious movement of
our day, and it was inevitable that, as Catholics and Protestants
began to talk openly with one another, much of this communication should take place in the pulpit. Across the land Catholic
and Protestant clergy are engaged in dialogues such as "The
Unity We Seek."

This sermon was preached in Westminster Presbyterian

Church, Portland, Oregon, on Reformation Sunday, October 25, 1964. It was the first time in Portland that any member of the Roman Catholic clergy had shared the pulpit in a Protestant church. The Rev. Paul E. Waldschmidt, the Roman Catholic partner who participated with Pastor Bonthius, writes of this experience:

> The congregation on October 25th was composed largely if not exclusively of members of Westminster Presbyterian Church. We presented the sermon in a dialogue fashion from two pulpits located on either side of the altar. From all reports and from the obvious interest and attention of the audience, I would say that the sermon was very well received. We prepared it by having a series of informal meetings and discussions, developing the topics. Then each of us wrote up the particular points he wished to make. A final meeting resulted in substantially the sermon . . . you have received. From my point of view, the discussions in preparation for the sermon were most stimulating and enlightening. It seems to me that it is through such experiences that real progress toward ecumenical understanding at least is to be made.

This dialogue illustrates the way contrasting points of view may be presented without making the style one of conflict. Pastor Bonthius and Father Waldschmidt intended to discuss Roman Catholic-Protestant differences in a spirit of unity with the aim of arriving at truth. They convey the image of understanding colleagues who support and encourage each other and have agreed to disagree only when necessary — in a spirit of love.

"THE UNITY WE SEEK"

Robert H. Bonthius and Paul E. Waldschmidt

Bonthius: It is a pleasure to welcome you into the life of this congregation and to this service of worship, Father Waldschmidt. It's going to be difficult for us not to fall into first names, because we work together in a number of community enterprises. I'd like to begin by clearing up one thing for the sake of the congregation. What does C.S.C. after your name stand for?

Waldschmidt: I certainly reciprocate your welcome. I am most
                grateful for the opportunity which your charity
                has brought about. It has been a pleasure to
                work with you in many civic affairs, and I am
                delighted to have the opportunity to discuss with
                you a matter of genuine concern to all of us. You
                asked about the C.S.C. It depends upon how
                friendly one is with me as to what it stands for.
                Some people speak of it as Can't Smoke Cigars,
                or City Street Cleaners, but students at the uni-
                versity generally say that it means: Cash, Son,
                Cash. Actually it is the Latin, *Congregatio a
                Sancta Cruce,* which means the congregation
                from Holy Cross. We are a French community
                that was founded in the little French town of
                Sainte Croix — Holy Cross — and we took our
                name from that. We are a group that assists
                parishes, assists priests, and also is engaged in
                the work of teaching. So C.S.C. has no really sin-
                ister meaning.

Bonthius: You know that in the Protestant church year this
                is Reformation Sunday. It seemed good to cele-
                brate the Reformation that is going on right now
                in the churches by scheduling this dialogue to-
                day. The keynote of the twentieth-century refor-
                mation seems to be the ecumenical movement,
                the movement through which the churches are
                trying to discover new unity. Now this means
                we are divided, else we wouldn't have to seek
                unity. I can tell you for Protestants that there is
                a real sense now of the sin of division. The first
                World Council of Churches meeting in Amster-
                dam in 1948 said this: "God has given to his
                people in Jesus Christ a unity which is His cre-
                ation and not our achievement . . . notwithstand-
                ing our divisions, we are one in Jesus Christ."
                But then it went on to say, "We confess that
                pride, self-will, and lovelessness . . . have played
                their part and still do" in our divisions. "We
                embark upon our world in the World Council of

Churches in *penitence* for what we are and in hope of what we may be."

Waldschmidt: I think that somewhat the same sentiments have been echoed by recent popes in expressing their sense of guilt as representatives of the Roman Catholic Church for the role that the Church had in bringing about the division of Christianity. It's rather significant, it seems to me, that at the very time of Luther, actually in 1522, the pope at that time, Adrian VI, sent his legates into Germany to preach to the people precisely the guilt that the Church recognized in itself. Pope Adrian's representatives recognized that the events surrounding Luther's denunciation of the abuses of the Church were "scourges of God upon the Church for its corruption and its wickedness." It's an unfortunate thing that it has taken so long for the entire Church to recognize guilt in the division of Christianity.

Bonthius: That's actually one thing that is making for unity, I think. It is the sense of responsibility that both Catholics and Protestants have for this division. Certainly Protestant historians are looking in a different way at the Reformation than they used to. As you see it, how are Roman Catholic thinkers viewing the Reformation now?

Waldschmidt: I think the most important thing is that now historians are viewing it not as Roman Catholic historians or Protestant historians. They are objectively considering the events that surround it. I can recall . . . that the Catholic was able to dismiss the entire Reformation by pointing out that Luther was an Augustinian monk who ran off with a woman, and this sort of solved the whole problem. It couldn't be anything of great value. A similar approach was taken with regard to the English Reformation. The emphasis was placed on the activity of Henry VIII and his desire to get rid of his wife, to divorce her and marry another.

Bonthius: And Luther married a nun, we might add.

Waldschmidt: Yes, you always bring in an extra little one! Even the Catholic historians didn't bring that up. The emphasis in other words was placed by our historians on moral character as they thought of the individuals who were responsible for the Reformation rather than on the problems, the basic issues that brought about the actual Reformation. The significant change is that today they are facing the issues.

Bonthius: I remember when the Protestant Reformation was taught to me as a repudiation of everything that the Roman Catholic Church stood for. Now the Reformation is being taught by historians in much less sweeping terms. They are pointing out that the Protestant Reformation retained much in Christian thought and Christian practice that had already been developed in the Catholic Church. For example, the doctrine of the Trinity, or the practices of baptism and the Lord's Supper. Historians are realizing that the Protestant Reformation of the sixteenth century was far more "Catholic" (quote/unquote) in its idea, for example, of the necessity of the church, or in its idea of the importance of the ordained ministry than later Protestantism seemed to remember. We now know that Luther and Calvin didn't want to start a "Protestant" (quote/unquote) church. They spoke constantly of reforming the Catholic Church. The very word Catholic was a word they used and cherished for the church.

Waldschmidt: As I see it in somewhat the same context as you have described, it seems to me that we'd be very rash if we tried to identify any one single factor as the cause of the Reformation. But I think it would be possible to point out a complexus of events or activities that could be considered as among the first causes of the Reformation. This could be summarized in the phrase that the

Reformation was brought about because of the desire to disentangle the spiritual from the temporal. In the time of Luther there is no question that the Catholic Church was involved almost inextricably in temporal affairs. The state was using the church for its purpose and vice versa. The bishops were also temporal rulers, and there was a great conflict between the church and the state for power. At the same time in this particular period of history a new nationalism was developing, the old society and the structure that had existed was changing so that both the church and the state were fighting not only each other for power but this other common enemy, the growing nationalism, the disintegration of empires, and so on. In such a setting it's quite easy to see how there could be quite a bit of corruption on the part of the clergy and how there could be expediency used instead of principle. The problem as I see it was this: there was a need for the Roman Church at this point in its history to reevaluate, to reaffirm, to reassess its role in society, but it was in such a position that it would not or could not do so without weakening itself with regard to the state or to the growing nationalism. So instead of doing the one thing that it should have done, it continued to reaffirm itself in its battle with the state and with the growing nationalism. My feeling is that there are certainly doctrinal differences which grew out of the Reformation, but I think that fundamentally these doctrinal differences grew because of a difference of understanding of the role of the Church in society, differences between the reformers and the Roman Church. This is the key, I think.

Bonthius: I suppose we could ask in the light of what we know now whether the Protestant Reformation was really necessary, but that would be purely academic. Surely we know one thing now about the Protestant Reformation and this is that it was never lacking in elements that have been retained by the Catholic Church. We also know that Catholicism contains many elements which are vital in the Protestant view of the Christian faith. Suppose we move on now to ask what factors besides this sense of common guilt for our division, what factors besides this reassessment of the Protestant Reformation are there that are bringing us together today?

Waldschmidt: In the Catholic Church I see the development of the concept of Catholic Action as a very important factor. It began with Pope Pius XI in 1850. Catholic Action was a call to the laity to more active participation in the apostolate, in the work of the hierarchy. It is significant that this call on the part of the pope was a recognition not only that the laity are more than just the masses to be ruled by the hierarchy. It was a return to a fundamental notion in the church that had been, somehow or other, lost sight of, or at least not given sufficient emphasis: that is the notion of the Church of Christ as a society of believers rather than an emphasis on the Church as only a highly structured, organized, hierarchical organization. This latter emphasis had prevailed; the former emphasis, the notion of the living church as the society of believers, this was not emphasized as much as it should have been. This call to Catholic action began the reemphasis on the role of the laity in the church as the living body of Christ.

Bonthius: That stress on the laity sounds very much like what Protestants call the priesthood of all believers, and I suspect that both of us would grant that this goes back clear to the Scripture itself. I was reading not long ago the book by the distinguished Dominican, Yves Congar, called *Lay People in the Church*. Father Congar points out that in the New Testament all Christians are called to be part of a "royal priesthood," as 1 Peter 2:9 puts it. Then Father Congar goes on to say that, while the idea of the holiness of the church in the past has been other-worldly, the idea of true spirituality is coming to be this-worldly. To use his words, true spirituality according to Scripture is "world-affirming rather than world-denying." It is significant that Catholic as well as Protestant leaders are studying the Bible, bringing its insights freshly to our attention, and emphasizing the importance of the laity. One of our own theologians, Hendrik Kraemer, has put it this way: "The laity are the frozen capital of the Church."

Waldschmidt: I'm glad to hear that they are the capital of the church. I noticed this morning in your announcement about the need for the congregation to bring its pledges up-to-date that we do have something very much in common in the Presbyterian Church and in the Roman Catholic Church!

Bonthius: Perhaps if we Protestant pastors put C.S.C. after our name we would get Cash, Son, Cash!

Waldschmidt: Seriously, your mention of Yves Congar recalls another factor that is very significant in helping to bring us together. That is the existence in Germany particularly and in the Alsatian or French University of Strasbourg of faculties of both Roman Catholic and Lutheran theology, with the result that there is an opportunity for continuing dialogue in these settings. In this regard it is significant that one of the leaders in the Roman Catholic Church today in the development of dogma, the doctrinal understanding of the church, is Hans Kung, who is a German theologian. Also, you alluded to the common study of Scripture. There has been greater collaboration between Protestant and Catholic and Jewish scholars in trying to understand and interpret the Scriptures. Joint work on the Dead

Sea Scrolls is an example. This has also had a tremendous influence on bringing about unity. It is significant again that one of the outstanding Catholic leaders in the ecumenical movement is Cardinal Bea. He has been a Scripture scholar. So that the theologian from Germany and a Scripture man epitomize these two factors which have had such a tremendous influence on beginning again this restoration of the body of Christ.

Bonthius: Something else we haven't mentioned that is contributing to unity is the experience on the mission fields of the various churches. First, among the Protestant churches there was great division. Each denomination was carrying on its own work in its own way in Asia and in Africa. Gradually the scandal of this division became apparent. There was overlapping, there was competition. So the churches began to cross denominational lines, they began learning what they had in common, they began to discover that some of their differences were due to ignorance or prejudice. This growing ecumenical emphasis in the mission field across the world has led Protestants to begin to think about their differences with Eastern Orthodoxy and Roman Catholicism. Protestants now know that prejudice and ignorance have accounted for part of the division there, and therefore they know that some differences can be overcome.

Waldschmidt: We've indicated most of the factors outside of the United States. They were such things as the development of Catholic Action, the emphasis on the role of the laity, Bible study among Christian scholars, European theological faculties, cooperation on the mission field. . . . There are certain elements here in our own country that have also helped to bring about this particular interest and desire for unity. Chief among them has been the development of the idea that Catholicism and democracy are compatible. This has happened in a period of forty years, between the campaign of the twenties with Al Smith, which was as you recall a very bitter and religious campaign, and the campaign in the sixties of John Kennedy, where religion had a part but not the significant part that it had in the twenties. In that span of forty years, I think that the idea that Catholicism is compatible with democracy became a part of the understanding of the American people. I believe this was done largely by the two Jesuit scholars, Father John Courtney Murray and Father Gustav Weigel. They did a tremendous service to us, to the church, and I think to the ecumenical movement, by helping to clarify the role of the church and state in a society such as this in America.

Bonthius: I knew you were going to mention Father Murray and Father Weigel, but I didn't think you would give a plug to the Jesuits.

Waldschmidt: Oh, we admit that they are Catholics.

Bonthius: Now these two men, Father Murray and Father Weigel, have done more to open my eyes to the possibility of more common ground between Catholics and Protestants than all the other factors we have mentioned rolled into one. When I was chaplain at Vassar some six to eleven years ago, there was very little dialogue between Catholics and Protestants going on. I was able to secure each of these theologians to lecture at Vassar for several days at a time. They made me realize that there was more than one way of reading the Catholic position on religious freedom. Since then, of course, Pope John XXIII has come out strongly for religious freedom in his encyclical, "Peace on Earth." I would like to read from that encyclical because it is a milestone in contemporary understanding of the Catholic view of religious liberty. Pope John wrote these words: One of the "rights of a human being" is "to honor God according to the sincere dictates of his own conscience." The pope went on to say that "the right to practice his religion privately and publicly" is a natural right of each man. I think this emphasis on religious liberty by the Catholic Church will probably do more for unity than any other single development in the twentieth century.

Waldschmidt: I quite agree, and I am glad you used the word "emphasis," for, as I see it as a Catholic theologian, the Catholic Church has always taught the absolute freedom of the act of faith. In other words, a person in his own conscience can only accept what he himself truly believes. He cannot be forced, he cannot be deprived by any external force, of his basic right to acknowledge his God as he sees it. This has been fundamental. I certainly don't want to minimize the serious complications that arose in certain countries in the application of this doctrine, but I do think that there has not been a sufficient understanding of the nature of this doctrine, and I thank God for Pope John with his idea of opening the windows of the church and letting a little bit of fresh air come in, letting a little bit of the dust blow off some of these doctrines so that we can see whether they really can be understood in the language of today. It is quite obvious that Catholics and Protestants have been talking to each other for four hundred years using perhaps the same language and the same words but certainly not having the same understanding. I think that the little formula that Pope John developed, the idea of concern, dialogue, and renewal provides us with a really excellent pattern as we try to achieve the unity we seek.

Bonthius: Indeed, we are doing some of that here — we have a concern for unity, we have a dialogue with regard to unity, and out of this we hope there will come a renewal of our understanding of what we have in common with each other

through Christ and what are our real differences.
I don't suppose any pope in modern times has
impressed Protestants the way Pope John did.
His benign countenance, his cheerfulness, his
charity, his championing of reforms endeared
him to the Protestant world. It would be hard to
imagine our standing here today in Christian
dialogue if it had not been for Pope John. However, when we go ahead now to talk about unity,
I think we need to define it. Everyone knows that
we're not one institutionally. Everyone knows
that we put our emphases on different aspects of
belief and practice. Yet, as the World Council
said at Amsterdam, "God has given to His people in Jesus Christ a unity which is His creation
and not our achievement." What then would you
say is the unity that we have?

Waldschmidt: Well, fundamentally I think that we would admit a unity of calling, that all of us are called to
be Christians, to be members of Christ's body.
This is a fundamental belief that we hold in
common. I was very impressed with the magnificent rendition of *The Credo* by your choir.
I'm looking forward to unity when we can get
that choir in the Catholic Church! I think we
could stand it. It was very lovely, and it was a
beautiful expression of what we hold in common. I think that the truths that are listed in
The Credo, these are fundamental, basic truths
that we accept. We are united in our baptism, in
our conviction of the Triune God, the Incarnation, redemption through Christ — these were all
listed for us and presented in a magnificent
fashion. So we have a basic unity of doctrine at
least in these truths.

Bonthius: And as we read in Ephesians this morning, we
have been "called in one hope of [our] calling,
one Lord, one faith, one baptism, one God and
Father of all" (Ephesians 4:4-6). I've been putting it this way recently with regard to the unity

that we have as being called in Christ. I've been saying that Protestants are finally discovering that Catholics are Christians, too! We have a certain unity of doctrine. We believe in Christ as the supreme revelation of God, we believe in the church as God's means of continuing to reveal himself to us, we believe in love as the law of the Christian life. We believe in the responsibility of Christians to work for justice in the world; all these things are bases of unity.

Waldschmidt: And, I think, your mention of the last one, working for justice, brings up another unity that has come about rather recently because of the opportunity to work together on civil rights problems. There has come an opportunity not only for Christians to work together but for Christians to work with their Jewish brothers in the effort to secure and guarantee civil rights for all men. This unity of social action is another unity that is a real one, and it should not be minimized to any extent.

Bonthius: Now if we have a unity of our calling, our common calling in Christ, and if we have a unity in doctrine up to a point, at least, and if we have a unity of social action, there is still that which keeps us apart. You and I have discussed this at length. Many, many theologians have done so. I am going to quote one of them. You might know that a Presbyterian would quote a Scotsman. Doctor Geddes MacGregor says that the real issue between us is the doctrine of the church. Doctor MacGregor says that is what the Reformation was about — more than about justification or grace. He contends that he and other Protestant theologians and Catholic experts like Father Yves Congar agree that the basic difference is the doctrine of the church. How do you respond to that?

Waldschmidt: I would respond in complete agreement. I think that in recent years there has been a considerable study of the understanding of justification and grace. Hans Kung's book, for example, was recognized by Karl Barth as a very good statement of the Barthian concept of grace and justification. I think that the real issue is the notion of the church, the nature of the church. We Catholics believe that the work of Christ was not completed with his resurrection or his ascension into heaven. It was his design that it continue until the end of the world. Christ promised to abide with those who believe in his name all days, even to the consummation of the world. Christ was going to remain with his followers, his church, until the end of the world. This I think we agree on. Where we differ, as I see it, is that we Catholics believe that out of this group of disciples who followed Christ he selected twelve whom we call apostles, and from this twelve he selected one, Peter, and to this group and their successors he gave the primary responsibility of preaching, teaching his revelation, and administering his sacraments or ordinances. So for us, an absolutely essential element in the church of Christ is this concept of apostolic succession. We see it as necessary for the integrity of doctrine and for the validity of sacramental orders. This, I think, is the fundamental difference.

Bonthius: This apostolic succession is found in the episcopate, that is, the bishops in union with the bishop of Rome, the Pope, and in matters of faith and morals. I believe that for you this episcopate, this apostolic succession, can define authoritatively faith and morals. Isn't that true? We Protestants also believe in apostolic succession. Our Westminster Confession of Faith, which is one of the standards of our church, puts it this way, the Holy Spirit works in the Church so that "the Church will be preserved, increased, purified, and at last made perfectly holy in the presence of God." The difference is that we don't

tie apostolic succession to a particular place or
office, such as the Bishops or the Pope. Fundamentally we believe that the Holy Spirit is ever
at work in and through the clergy of the church
but not in such a way that the clergy is preserved
from making mistakes in matters of faith and
morals. I rather hate to say this, but, in our view,
the laity may have to correct the clergy! And the
laity themselves need correction. In short, we
have no such group as a college of bishops in the
church, which can be said to be infallible.

Waldschmidt: I think that is a very good statement of our precise difference. But again it seems to me that
there is much room in it for more clarification
and for greater understanding because the term
"infallibility" has become a red flag to many who
are outside the church, and I think that it needs
to be understood. We are saying by "infallibility"
that it is Christ's aim or purpose to see to it that
the church, when it is believing or accepting his
revelation, is going to be protected so that it will
not accept as his revelation what is not truly his
revelation. I think that you could go along with
this, from what I gather. For you have said that
the Holy Spirit is acting in the church. We
would agree that what we Catholics try to do is
to find where we might locate, so to speak, this
particular action of infallibility. Our sources of
revelation are Scripture and tradition. These are
the sources of our faith. This is where we find
what Christ has revealed. Now how do we know
that we understand properly what Christ has
revealed? We believe that Christ has established
a means whereby this will be guaranteed, namely
his abiding presence with the church. Where
is that presence? We see it as located first of all
in the entire church, the laity, and the bishops,
and the pope, so that what they all believe in
common on a matter that is contained in either
Scripture or tradition, this (if they are proposing

it as a divine revelation) is divine revelation preserved from error. We find infallibility in the
common consensus of all the bishops proposing
as divine revelation something that is contained
in Scripture or tradition. We find it lastly in the
pope himself or in conjunction with his council.
The difference between us is that we have tried
to say where we could find an infallible authority
that is presenting to us as revelation what Christ
reveals.

Bonthius: I think this problem of *location* is really central
to our discussion. For us as Protestants there is
only one infallible authority, and that is Jesus
Christ, the word made flesh. Though through his
spirit we believe he guides the church. But we
cannot find in any individual or group of human
beings, even though they are guided by Jesus
Christ, those whom we would regard as infallible.
To put it clearly by going to the other extreme
from Catholicism, let us refer to fundamentalist
Christianity. . . . [Many fundamentalists] declare
that they and they alone have the truth, they and
they alone understand the Scripture. Scripture is
infallible, they understand Scripture, so they are
infallible. This is a quite un-Protestant position.
For us, the pronouncements and the practices of
any ecclesiastical authority, whether fundamentalist Protestant or Roman Catholic or any other
group, ought to be challenged from time to time.
Let me give an example. Martin Luther King, in
his letter from a Birmingham jail, was responding to eight clergymen who disapproved of his
action. Now it is interesting that Dr. King used
the Bible as his authority. He also used tradition.
He cited Aquinas and Augustine, Martin Luther
and John Bunyan, along with many others, to
make it clear that they too were willing to be imprisoned, if necessary, for the sake of justice, and
to make it clear that men must protest against
the church's failure to stand boldly for racial

justice. But, in the last analysis, Dr. King had to stand up to those ecclesiastical officials and say, as Peter did hundreds of years before him, "We must obey God rather than man!" (Acts 5:29). Perhaps, when the chips are down, it is this divine right of individual dissent in relationship to Scripture and tradition, in relation to all councils of church and state, that is so typically Protestant.

Waldschmidt: I think that's very true. But again, there's a question. I don't want to keep going back to this idea of emphasis, but it strikes me, as we've discussed this for many hours together, that even in the Protestant churches you do recognize a permanence of doctrine. There are certain truths that you professed in your creed this morning. Now a layman could come up and challenge you with regard to whether or not Christ was made incarnate. Would the Presbyterian Church change? I don't think so. I think you hold that the Holy Spirit is protecting you, that this is a revealed truth that you will hold on to. We would admit the necessity of the laity to correct the clergy in their own personal differences, in their own moral conduct, in their own deviation from doctrinal truth. We would also hold that the laity can correct the church in the sense of bringing to it an understanding of revelation as given in Scripture and in tradition. This certainly can be done. And I wonder if it isn't again a question of emphasis. We hold that the Catholic Church must continue to work for a deeper and more profound understanding of Christ's revelation, and you believe this too. We are doing this through the laity, through the bishops, through the councils, and so on, trying to understand Christ's doctrine. For example, the liturgy has been developed. It is not changeless. The liturgy can be and is being changed now. The only fundamental thing that we would have to retain in our mass is the actual words of consecration whereby we believe the bread and the wine become the body of Christ. Everything else in the mass has been added. It could be dropped today. As a matter of fact, we have to look at the paper every morning to find out if they did! Things are happening rather rapidly. The idea, though, of something that is permanent, guaranteed, and protected — this is our notion of infallibility, and of the role of these leaders in our church. And it seems to me that this exists in your church also to some extent.

Bonthius: With these twin emphases on certain basic truths which are the very basis of our Christian faith, and the need constantly to hold our understanding of these truths under judgment and correction, it may very well be that we are striving for a new language — a language that is not the language either of us has used so far, but that will one day emerge and adequately express these twin emphases on the truth that is given to us, and our need constantly to correct our understanding in the fullness of this truth. I wonder where we go from here. Do you think that we have reached all the unity that we possibly can reach?

Waldschmidt: Well, I don't think so, no. I think that we have somewhat demonstrated it in our dialogue this morning. Certainly we have demonstrated it to our own satisfaction in our private dialogues. We have found that the ideas we had of one another's doctrines were not adequate. We have found that we need to ask each other and ourselves why we are holding what we profess to hold, and whether or not we really understand what the other person is holding. We need to reassess the validity for the various truths that are being presented. And I think from the Catholic point of view it's always been a source of real amazement to me that those who were not

members of the Catholic Church take as infallible practically everything that comes out of the
Catholic Church, whether by a bishop or a priest
or whoever it might be, that this is somehow
or other an infallible doctrine. Actually, we've
got only a handful of things that we would profess as being defined by the church as revelation
and therefore infallibly true. I think that part of
the difficulty is a lack of precision and clarification on our part in presenting to those who are
not of the Catholic Church what we mean when
we say this is an infallible truth. We need to
make it clear that some things that are in the
church can certainly change. I think we need the
same appreciation of Protestantism. For us, Protestantism is a fragmented group of people who
hold contradictory doctrines. Some say that
Christ is God, some say not. Some say this
is the Eucharist, some say it is not. For us,
we have not made any effort to try to find
out what Protestants believe. Are there real
basic differences in understanding? Or are our
differences more in the way we formulate our
doctrines? We Catholics have simply lumped
all Protestants together; well, they are all contradictory, and it's such a mess we can't understand it at all, so we might as well leave them.
This is wrong, and this has been the attitude
of the Catholic Church, I think, to a great extent, Catholic theologians, not the Catholic
Church. I'm one of the boys that lumped them.

Bonthius: Well, we all lump, I think, and this suggests to
me the statement made by a great Protestant
churchman who said that the twentieth century
reformation is as radical, that is to say, as deeply
probing of the roots of our faith as was the sixteenth century, and we are just at the beginning
of this reformation.

Waldschmidt: I think this is very true. Actually, as far as the
Catholic Church is concerned, we were not re-

formed in the sixteenth century. The activities of the Council of Trent which has been characterized as the Counter Reformation, these activities were designed to root out the causes or the abuses which existed in the church, and in order to do this it was necessary that they make stronger and stricter rules so that the church became even more rigid, more formalized than before. Christopher Dawson has stressed this point, and it has always made a great impression on me, that our modern world was beginning to develop in this sixteenth century, the new epic was beginning, and at this very point Christianity was engaged in a civil war so that this new world was developing without the guidance, without the influence of Christianity. We in the Catholic Church, and I think in most of the Protestant churches also, we are beginning this *aggiornamento,* as Pope John called it, this updating; we are bringing the thing up to date, we are trying to bring Christ, the incarnate Christ into our modern world, into the twentieth century, and take Christian doctrine and apply it to the twentieth century. I think that for this reason we are celebrating Reformation Sunday, we are celebrating it as an historical event. I think also we are celebrating it as a prophetic event, because reformation is just beginning as I see it, really.

Bonthius: We might well end with the Apostle's word that we must learn, as he says in Ephesians 4:15, to "speak the truth in love" so that we may "grow up in every way into him who is the head, into Christ." We know that we have much growing to do before the churches become the community of faith that God intends.

Thank you, Father Waldschmidt. Through you we have experienced some of that growth in love this morning.

DIALOGUE OF INQUIRY:
"NO FURTHER TREK"

THIS SERMON was preached on October 23, 1966, at University Methodist Church, Syracuse, New York, by the pastor of that church, Robert H. Bolton, and a Methodist colleague, Harlan London. University Church, located in a downtown predominantly Negro neighborhood, is a church of 900 members. However, the congregation consists mainly of white middle-class business and professional people and members of the university community.

Robert Bolton describes the genesis and development of this particular dialogue:

> I became pastor of the church less than four months before the sermon was preached. The sermon title was announced in the weekly newsletter and there was no intention of it being a dialogue sermon. My friend, Harlan London, stopped by to talk about another matter. I picked his brains about the forthcoming sermon on race relations. His ideas were so good—and so well expressed—that it seemed he should give the sermon, not I. But even if he gave it, it seemed people might hear only his words and not his message.
>
> Suddenly the thought occurred—why not start the sermon as I planned and have Harlan interrupt me from the floor and come to the pulpit to make his remarks. I would ask him some questions from time to time.
>
> The congregation that worshiped in the lovely Gothic church which has some of the loveliest stained glass windows in the East, was shocked and electrified when a tall stranger, a Negro, stood up and suddenly challenged their pastor in the middle of his sermon. An usher thought, "It's my duty to protect the pastor." One parishioner said, "After he interrupted you I didn't hear another word, but a few days later this message dawned on me. The only way the Negro gets a chance to be heard in our society is to interrupt what is already going on." Most of the people were led by his logic to agree with Mr. London's ideas. A few expressed disagreement with parts of it—especially what they thought he was saying about black power. All were thoughtful. It forced everyone to think, and feel, more than any sermon had in a long time.

The Reverend Harlan London is a Methodist minister who serves under special appointment as Protestant Chaplain to the

Onondaga County Family Court and Hillbrook Detention Home, a service provided by the Syracuse Area Council of Churches.

"NO FURTHER TREK"

Harlan London and Robert Bolton

Minister: When Abraham left Haran on the Euphrates River to search for a more relevant religion and a finer way of life, his nephew Lot was at his side. They journeyed across parched deserts of desolate wilderness before reaching their destination in Palestine. At journey's end they were disappointed to find a place in the paralyzing grip of famine. The weary pilgrims were forced to trek on until they found green pastures for their cattle and abundant riches for themselves. An unfortunate experience with the Pharoah, however, caused their expulsion from that land. The hardy adventurers returned to the "Holy Land," where they continued to prosper.

After they dwelt in the land of promise for some time, there developed "strife between the herdsmen of Abraham's cattle and the herdsmen of Lot's cattle" (Genesis 13:7). The two leaders were concerned about the persistent conflict. One day the aged patriarch took his nephew to a bluff which afforded a view of the surrounding territory. As they surveyed the lands spread out before them, Abraham demonstrated a magnanimity which is almost unmatched in the long annals of history. "Let there be no strife between you and me, and between your herdsmen and my herdsmen: for we are kinsmen," he exclaimed. "Is not the whole land before you? Separate yourself from me. If you take the land to the left, I will go to the right, or if you go to the right land, I will go to the left."

Lot's response to this spirit of generosity was disappointing. His actions can be characterized by one word: greed. He saw that the Jordan Valley was well watered and looked like "a garden of the Lord." Lot took all of the best land and the two friends parted.

I would like to lift up two related truths that are suggested by this Biblical narrative. The first is self-evident; that this was one of Abraham's finest hours. He had not always acted so nobly (Genesis 12:11ff.). In this moment, however, his magnificent magnanimity is unquestioned. He, the tribal elder, could undoubtedly have kept the best portion of the land for himself. Instead, in an act of almost reckless abandon, he offered Lot his choice and the younger man made the most of the opportunity. In this incident, we see the character of Abraham at its best.

The second insight grows out of the first. Even when he was at his best, Abraham did not find the most constructive way of dealing with interpersonal conflict. Instead of solving interpersonal problems, he evaded them. We must not let his generosity cloud the issue. Underneath all of the sugar-coated generosity was bitter hostility. "Separate yourself from me," he demanded, and "they separated from each other" (13:9, 11).

Abraham tried to solve the problem of human relationships by evasion, and that pattern has normally been followed throughout history.

When I was in South Africa in 1963, it was evident that the separation which Abraham demanded was the pattern which that nation had chosen. In the early years, the Afrikaaners could not get along with the English, so they trekked into the interior and developed that part of the nation. The Voortrekkers handled intercultural conflict by the strategy of separation. They were heroic, self-reliant, and devout people. They were admirable in many ways which are enshrined in the history and folklore of their nation. But their solution of human conflict was inadequate, and the apartheid philosophy which has grown out of the earlier "solution" is despicable.

The problems which impede the achievement of real brotherhood today are far greater than they were in the time of Abraham. P. V. Pistorius, a South African intellectual, writes: "It is no longer merely a question of quarrels between shepherds over the best grazing. Other factors far more vague and consequently far more complex have made their appearance. Today we speak of things like a way of living, national character, traditions, language, and a host of other things. We are barnacled by the injustices we have suffered and the injustices we have inflicted on those who are equally barnacled in relation to us. Abraham and Lot started from scratch and failed to solve their problems. We are overloaded with handicaps and yet we dare no longer evade the issue." [1]

We cannot dodge the interpersonal issues any more, because with transportation shrinking the globe and the population explosion overcrowding it there are no longer enough open spaces. Any further trek would be impossible.

> Now the frontiers are all closed,
> There is no other country we can run away to.
> There is no ocean we can cross over.
> At last we must turn and live with one another. . . .
> Love is no longer a theme for eloquence, or a way of
>   life for a few to choose whose hearts can decide it,
> It is the sternest necessity; the unequivocal ultimatum.
> There is no other way out; there is no country we can flee
>   to,
> There is no man on earth who must not face this task
>   now.[2]

---

[1] P. V. Pistorius, *No Further Trek* (Johannesburg, South Africa: Central News Agency Limited, 1957) , p. 5.

[2] Peggy Pond Church, "Ultimatum," *Fellowship*, April, 1949 (Nyack, N.Y.: The Fellowship of Reconciliation) .

Since evasion is no longer feasible, let us turn from the tactics of Abraham to the strategy of the New Testament. Instead of dealing with strife by separation, the New Testament urges reconciliation. It insists on confrontation in love.

The book of Ephesians alludes to the alienation and hostility which is felt by one group of people toward another. It pictures the barriers that separate people. Then it gives the solution to the hatred which has marred our life together. It informs us that Christ "is our peace, who has made us both one, and has broken down the dividing wall of hostility" (Ephesians 2:14). In these words we find the way of the tangled web of —

Interrupter: (A TALL NEGRO STRANGER WHO STANDS UP SUDDENLY IN THE MIDST OF THE CONGREGATION) But Reverend Sir! That's fine, but can't we take these teachings from the Scriptures and make them speak of the problems we face in our time and in our community? (INTERRUPTER MOVES UP TO THE PULPIT) Sure, we can talk of Abraham's trying to solve the problem of human relationships by evasion, but to leave it there will only reinforce us in our thinking that this is the way in which we must solve our own problems in human relationships. We have in our own experience the alienation and hostility felt by one group toward another — the power structure of this country must finally come to realize that racial unrest and peaceful solutions to this problem cannot come until we deal with these influences undermining peace. The federal government will eventually be forced to protect the peace and individual rights of all citizens, regardless of race, creed, or color, in order to project and protect its image abroad. But until that time comes, the American Negro must continue to push and fight this battle at home.

Reverend, there can be no let-up. Can't we speak of this?

Minister: You are right in insisting that we get down to specific cases. Can you describe for us what is the impact of prejudice on family life?

Interrupter: I suppose it is easy for those who have never felt the sting of rejection and segregation to feel that Negroes should not think of the effect of the race problem on family life, but when I experience the humiliation of hate-filled policemen cursing Negro children; and when I suddenly find myself stammering to explain to my five-year-old daughter what the demonstrations are all about; and when I see the depressing cloud of inferiority begin to veil itself over her mental sky and her personality become resistive toward those who created it, I am left with no choice but to face up to the realities of those questions and offer some explanation. When my daughter came to me and said "Daddy, am I black?" I replied, "Yes." Not satisfied with this answer because of the emotional meaning which was conveyed when she was told this by her friends, she turned to her mother, "Mamma, am I black?" Her mother replied, "Yes." Seemingly, she was convinced that this was a fact which she must accept. Several days following this experience, my daughter and I watched the March on Washington. She wanted to know the meaning of this, and after my explanation of this address of grievances, she remarked, "Daddy, isn't it sad? It just makes me want to cry because it has to be done." These illustrations only emphasize the internal problems of child rearing and what influences the problem of race has on the mind of the young child.

Within the context of education, my nine-year-old son five years ago was asked by his teacher to join another child in his classroom to erase the blackboard. Upon completion of his share of this task and in his attempt to return to his seat, he slightly bumped the girl who was erasing the other part of the blackboard. When this happened, she said, "Don't touch me, black boy." The class of students became enraged at this and urged my son to feel angry. The teacher replied, "You should be ashamed, Mary. How would you like someone to say something like that to you; after all, your folks are not from this country either."

Reverend, we have a long way to go in overcoming barriers to acceptance which prejudice brings to the Negro family.

Minister: I am forced to agree that you are right. Prejudice which hurts children like that should be stopped. But don't you feel that a change of heart must come first, if race relations are to be improved?

Interrupter: The oppressor will never voluntarily change his or her heart and be converted or awakened to relieve the burdens or problems of the oppressed. History has proven this. I often hear the expression, "I want to do the right thing but I don't know what I can do." I refuse to believe our lack of knowledge is due to any serious limitation in methods, but rather our failure to want to know; the failure of intention and will. We don't act because we really don't want to have a change of heart. Laws can help change the problems of legislation affecting the lives of the Negro on the job, in the classroom, and where he wishes to live. Laws cannot control prejudice, but can aid in the control of open defiance to justice. Laws cannot control or legislate man's moral obligation, but can provide a framework to deal with man's immoralities. To give an illustration, in 1962 my family attempted to be accommodated at one of the chain of motels in Memphis, Tennessee. The reservation clerk, when asked if the motel could accommodate a family of four, turned and said to the janitor, "Johnny, can you tell these people where they can find a place to stay?" — never answering my original question. We were not accommodated in Memphis, and we decided to continue the hundred-mile journey to where our family lives. In 1964, after the Public Accommodation Act was then passed, the manager of this same chain of motels made public his attitude, the gist of which was, "At last we can do what I wanted to do for a long time, but could not because I was bound by local tradition." Reverend, laws can help change established traditions and relieve the consciences of people who want to act but are bound by tradition set by the power structure.

Minister: As you speak of change that occurred between 1962 and 1964, I cannot help but think of the tremendous progress which has been accomplished in the past few years. Why are Negroes pressing so hard for even more radical change? Wouldn't it be better if we move slowly and surely?

Interrupter: We need to truly repent before we can assess the progress which has been made or assess the need for acceleration. Our pride and satisfaction with present gains can easily lead to lethargy. It is not enough to throw a few goodies of justice to the Negro and think the problem has been solved. This has been a traditional way of responding which causes no suffering or transformation, and only reinforces the prevailing feelings of superiority. Here we need to establish what repentance is — it is not feeling sorry (e.g., wasn't it too bad about those children who were bombed in the church in Alabama, or wasn't it too bad about Dr. Spike's death?). Statements like these can be made without a sense of feeling or involvement, and are useless. Repentance begins with a feeling of intense horror for the violation . . . of human dignity; reliving the incident; an awareness of what has been done to another person, with some positive steps to alleviate the problem which caused it. There are people, Reverend, who feel intensely identified with the problem of the Negro who are seeking to act responsively; but, sad to say, we need more commitment and action.

Minister: Your talk about spiritual matters like repentance seems to contrast strongly with the phrase "Black Power" that we hear so much today. Can you explain your understanding of this phrase?

Interrupter: I cannot talk about POWER without making a few points about both BLACK POWER and the WHITE POWER structure. Whatever names are given to the structures of society — whether they are BLACK POWER or WHITE POWER — the simple message is that God has not ordained any small group of men to hold power over all the others. He chose his most powerful leaders from among the ranks of the humble, and when they became proud and pompous, He put them aside as unworthy.

This problem hits us at the most sensitive nerve of our nation today, as we hear words by one of the keenest analysts of urban life, Harvey Cox:

> . . the powerlessness of oppressed peoples is the key issue. The real illness of the American city today, and especially of the deprived groups within it, is voicelessness, the lack of either the readiness, the capacity, or the channels to make their legitimate needs felt throughout the whole system.[3]

This is to say that power is centralized in our social system; some of it necessarily to provide representative government, some of it preferentially to protect special interests and prejudices.

As in all centuries before this one, men will continue to rush on in the search for power. Some will call it "Black Power," when they mean the yielding of the power structure to include the black man within that structure. Others will come back with pious calls for spiritual power without recognizing that we are called, if not condemned, to life in the world of real men with problems of dignity, respect, love, life, and death. Still others will long for the kind of utopias in which all are powerless, never knowing that it is the land of the dead.

Freedom from this dilemma comes from the recognition that power belongs to God, who calls us into responsible stewardship of its possession and use. We become so used to reserving power for

[3] Harvey Cox, *The Secular City* (New York: The Macmillan Company, 1966), p. 116.

those who are in position to wield it that we forget that even the humblest man has the power to say "No" to some of the powers he is asked to condone. We become so used to thinking of our power to conquer, rather than thinking of our power to reconcile and redeem. All persons are creatures of God; therefore, the center of God's power can flow through us and cause us to be what we can become. Our Christian faith speaks against the accumulation of power and might that is used to the detriment of the poor, the lonely, and the dispossessed. God has not chosen people to exercise their power. He chose us to be responsible stewards of its possession and use. So, when we pray, ". . . Thine is the Power . . ." we are not resigning but rather acknowledging the source of life's creative force and purpose — God with us and working through us to fulfill his purpose.

DIALOGUE OF CONFLICT: "PREACHER MEETS HIPPIE"

THIS SERMON is a good example of a conflict-dialogue in which the conflict is partially resolved. Written in modern idiom and delivered in a breezy conversational manner, this dialogue uses the hippie phenomenon to focus sharply on the meaning of love and, in particular, the factors of feeling and action. Certainly the conclusion to the sermon is dramatic; in their joint flower-passing act the preacher and the hippie demonstrate that there is a reconciling power in love which can build bridges between the most diverse elements of society.

D. Richard Hepler, a graduate of an American Baptist seminary, is now serving as a social worker in a Detroit housing project. This dialogue was presented in a Sunday morning worship service at Friendship House, an American Baptist Christian Center in Hamtramck, Michigan, for an audience composed largely of young people below the age of sixteen. Mr. Hepler indicates that the feedback following the presentation suggested that many were unable to comprehend the idea-content, and that this dialogue might be more effective with an older, more sophisticated audience.

The intent of the sermon was to create a conflict, dramatize ideas, and resolve the conflict to some degree but with each character maintaining his identity and integrity throughout. To accomplish these ends, costuming made the characters easily identifiable; the preacher wore a clerical robe, and the hippie was arrayed in offbeat apparel. Although the minister was interrupted by the hippie, who was located at the rear of the sanctuary, the congregation had been given some advance warning that the sermon would be unusual.

"PREACHER MEETS HIPPIE"

D. Richard Hepler

Preacher: The title of this morning's sermon is —

Hippie: (COMING FROM THE REAR OF THE CONGREGATION) Hey, Preacher, I would like to say something! I took a trip last night and I want to tell everybody about it.

Preacher: (NOTICEABLY DISTURBED) Sir! I mean, young man! Well, whoever you are, I am not accustomed to being interrupted during my sermon, and furthermore, no one is permitted to speak before this congregation unless they are dressed properly.

Hippie: Now look, preach, don't go makin' remarks about my apparel.

Preacher: Well, after all, you must admit that it is a little weird. Most people don't go around dressed like that.

Hippie: Man, you've got a lotta room to talk. I don't see very many people dressed like you.

Preacher: I'll have you to know, young man, that this robe distinguishes me as a man of the cloth, a minister of the church.

Hippie: Like man, my rags distinguish me too, don't they?

Preacher: Enough of this talk about clothing. Since you've already disrupted the worship service, you may as well say what you wanted to say so that we can get on with the service.

Hippie: I'm very sorry about cutting into your time like this but I was really turned on last night. Man, like I took this trip and I heard my blood rushing through my veins. I saw colors I've never seen before. It was like feeling, seeing, and hearing everything at once! It was like being at one with everything and everybody. I wanted to embrace the whole world with love. I wanted to conquer the world with love. I wanted to zap everybody with love.

Preacher: Well, sir, I guess you know that you are stealing my lines. I'm the one that's supposed to be saying "Conquer the world with love." Anyway, what do you know of love? Your idea of love is a pleasure-seeking love of the flesh. I've read about you people. You live together and have all kinds of illicit relations with one another. And, God knows what takes place at those love-ins you've been conducting!

Hippie: Man, you are really "straight." You're so hung up on your moralistic mumbo-jumbo you couldn't love if you wanted to. You're so afraid of your feelings of love that you suppress them. You can't love because you're afraid to.

Preacher: You talk as though love is just a feeling. But love is more than that! Love is an act. Love has no meaning unless one does something to help another person.

Hippie: So you say love is an act. Well, if love is doing, where are all the lovers? Like man, everybody is so busy grabbing for himself that he doesn't have time to help anyone else. Everybody wants to get to the top and he'll climb right over anyone who is in front of him. This so-called Christian nation should be full of lovers but instead it's overpopulated with grabbers. Christ was a groovy cat but unfortunately no one got the message. Nobody really tuned in and got turned on.

Preacher: Yes, but Christ was a doer. He did acts of love.

Hippie: Sure, but he had to feel loving before he could act. Anyway, on both counts you cats are losers. You don't feel or act love.

Preacher: By the way, what gives you the right to act as judge and jury over us?

Hippie: Like man, I'm a dropout. I dropped out of your society a long time ago. You cats don't show me nothin'. You've been at it for several thousand years and look what you've accomplished — nothing! You're always talking about makin' this a better world to live in. You babble about creating the kingdom of God on earth. And, what do you have to show for all your efforts? Nothin'. And now L.B.J. has introduced the Great Society — the biggest lie of all. Who are you trying to kid, anyway? Like man, it'll never happen! Who am I to judge? I'm the only one with a right to judge, because I'm no longer a member of your society.

Preacher: You say that you have dropped out. Yet you continue to live on this planet and to take advantage of numerous public facilities, such as parks for your love-in. I think perhaps you drop out only when it is to your advantage or liking.

Hippie: You just don't understand, man. Your style of life, mores, and morals have turned us off completely. We may occupy the same space, but we're "spaced," out of communication with each other.

Preacher: Also, I've thought it peculiar that you and yours are so critical of my incapacity to love, and yet you indulge in drugs in order to acquire a state of euphoria. You apparently need drugs so that you can love!

Hippie: You're really in a straitjacket, man. Who cares how you acquire the love feeling so long as it happens to you?

Preacher: Yes, but what of the consequences? What happens when LSD causes psychotic after-effects?

Hippie: The trouble with you straights is that you don't know anything about drugs and you always exaggerate the after-effects.

Preacher: Furthermore, drugs don't really alter or change one's basic personality, so when you return from a trip you are the same person as you were before you left: the kind of person who is very much like his predecessor, his forefathers. It seems to me that you are deceiving yourself as you have been deceived by your forebearers. You know, I'm willing to concede that your idea of love has merit, and, in fact, love is a thought, feeling, and action basic to the Christian faith. But, I still believe that you overemphasize the feeling aspect of love. There is no love without action.

Hippie: Yes, but by the same token there is no love without feeling. If love is only action, then it is a big act. It's a fake. Anyone who acts without feeling is a con artist and the world is full of charlatans. You know, that's what bugs me about you guys. You try to act without feeling and you become sterile do-gooders.

Preacher: You make your point very well. We often act without any sincere, genuine feeling for the person we intend to help. Granted, we must feel before we act, but the loving process is not complete unless we act. And it seems to me that this is where your philosophy is faulty. You talk about loving everybody and at the same time drop out, withdraw from society. You establish your own subculture, your own communities where you love and take care of your own. That's fine. But by withdrawing you are not really challenged to act in a loving manner toward others. You talk about love, but you are not challenged to act in love in difficult circumstances.

Hippie: Man, you are really out of touch. What about the beatings we've taken at the hands of the cops? We've acted in love toward them. We've even planned picnics for their children. What more do you expect?

Preacher: Such behavior is commendable. However, I think there is a difference. That kind of love-acting borders on sensationalism. You see, the hippie community shelters and protects you from the everyday problems and conflicts which other people face. You drop out and therefore don't have to cope. You are really not challenged to act in love.

Hippie: Say man, what are you trying to do? Convert me?

Preacher: No, but I thought perhaps you were attempting to convert me.

Hippie: (LAUGHING) Are you kidding, man? You're much too straight.

Preacher: Don't you think this apparel could gain some points for me?

Hippie: Like man, you might score a few points but you'll never make it. You're in a red, white, and blue straitjacket. You're bound up with all the acceptable middle-class American values. Furthermore, you still believe that the American and/or Christian dream can come true. Like man, forget it. Those are fantasies which will never come true regardless of how hard you work on them.

Preacher: In spite of all our disagreements, I think we can agree on one thing, at least: each one of us believes that the other is in a fantasyland. You believe my style of life is a foolish fantasy, and I think yours is a dull dream.

Hippie: We certainly are "spaced," man. But say, didn't we agree that there is no love without feeling? Honest, genuine love is rooted in feeling. What do you say to that?

Preacher: I'll buy it. What do you say about the *acting* aspect of love?

Hippie: I think I can buy that, too, even though you don't understand or appreciate my acts of love. Say, let's cut out the chatter. I didn't come here for a philosophical discussion, anyway. I just came here to super-zap everyone with love! Love . . . love . . . (AS HE BEGINS TO PASS OUT FLOWERS TO CONGREGANTS) . . . .

Preacher: May I join you?

Hippie: By all means, man. (HE HANDS SEVERAL FLOWERS TO THE PREACHER, AND THE TWO WALK TO THE REAR OF THE SANCTUARY PASSING OUT FLOWERS.)

DIALOGUE OF CONFLICT: "INS AND OUTS"

THIS HAUNTING INTERPRETATION of a familiar parable was preached by the Rev. Vern Campbell and Elder Fred Libbey on October 9, 1966, in the Peoples Presbyterian Church of Milan, Michigan. In the dialogue, the pastor represented the "Ins" and the layman represented the "Outs." Mr. Campbell indicates that Mr. Libbey is a very articulate Christian who wrote his own part in the sermon after they had spent several sessions together analyzing the parable and the concepts within it. The sermon was delivered from a script at a regular Sunday morning service, and it seemed to be well received by the congregation.

This sermon is unique in that the participants are not diametrically opposed, despite their representing the in-group and the out-group of society. On one level, the two voices support each other in their common affirmation that Christians must be socially sensitive. On another level, conflict develops as the Voice of the Outs vigorously attacks the other's hypocrisy and reveals the lethargy and indifference that lies just beneath the surface of their lives. The language used is vivid, and the Voice of the Outs conjures up some poignant scenes to justify his despair and bursting frustration.

Notice that the Voice of the Ins fails to make any direct reply to his accuser; in fact, he takes little notice of the other person until the end of the sermon, when they join in a brief and extremely provocative prayer that would keep the congregation pondering its meaning for days. But perhaps it is the fact that he is ignored by the in-group that is most aggravating to the Voice of the Outs; and this symbolic presentation of bitter frustration in the face of an Establishment which fails to treat him personally would relate significantly to many people in the audience.

"INS AND OUTS"

Vern Campbell and Fred Libbey

Scripture: Leviticus 16:6-10 (READ BY VOICE OF THE OUTS, ELDER FRED LIBBEY)

Matthew 25:31-46 (READ BY VOICE OF THE INS, REV. VERN CAMPBELL)

Voice of the Ins: In the parable of the Last Judgment as recorded in the 25th chapter of Matthew, Jesus is pictured as a judge. In his role as judge he separates. He separates one from the other — the sheep from the goats — the good from the bad — the ins from the outs. In this day, the extension of Christ, which is his church, is engaged in the same kind of judgment. We of the church, as his body, still exercise the powers of division. We separate. We determine the good and the bad. We decide who is on the inside and who is on the outside.

In Jesus' day, and with the figures he used, it was not a difficult decision to make. For the Syrian sheep he spoke of were usually white, and the goats were black. So, you see the idea of white hats and black hats really is not new! Certainly Jesus was aware that the evaluation of a person is very complex. It is not black and white. It is a decision to make about variations in shades of grey. It is very difficult to describe the ins or the outs. Drawing a line between the good and the evil is not a simple matter. Who are the sheep? What are they like? Well, if we take Jesus seriously in this parable, then we cannot take seriously the

129

method we generally employ to make our judgments. We separate upon the basis of nationality. We ask, "Is he American?" We separate upon the basis of race. We ask, "Is he Negro?" We separate upon the basis of religion. We ask, "Is he Presbyterian?" Not so with Jesus. He mentions only one criterion. The sheep are those who feed the hungry, give drink to the thirsty, welcome the stranger, clothe the naked, and visit the sick and those imprisoned. It is a matter of behavior. This describes the "Ins," the sheep who sit on the right hand.

Voice of the Outs: As a sophisticated congregation, it cannot have escaped your attention that I am not sitting on the right hand of God, but on the left. This is quite deliberate. I delivered to you also a message from the book of Leviticus, wherein we are explained. It is a psychological principle that we all need someone to drive into the desert, to bear upon his back our transgressions. It is for those driven into the desert that I will speak. For the hungry. For the thirsty. For the stranger and the exiled. For the naked and sick and the imprisoned. We have generally made them inarticulate. We have words for them. We have said "outs." They are exiles. Pariahs. Ostracized. The scapegoats. But you cannot escape the message which says we do not really know who will be driven into the desert, who will finally be the goats. I speak for them. For they are not here.

Voice of the Ins: Disconcerting as it may be, the "Ins" need the "Outs." The saved need the unsaved. For if everyone were saved, how would we know it? The "Outs" are required to tell us who is in. In short, we need evil. The sheep need goats, to know they are sheep.

In our parable both the sheep and the

goats ask the question, "Lord, when did we see thee?" Neither of them thought they had seen the Lord, but the difference was that the sheep were sensitive to human need and the goats were not. And the story is completed with the line from the lips of the shepherd judge: "Truly I say to you, as you did it to one of the least of these my brethren, you did it to me." What did they do? "Lord, when did we see you?"

"I was hungry, and you gave me food." Man is always hungry; from the time of his conception to the moment of his death, he hungers. His physical body requires nourishment. His spiritual being cries out for satisfaction. The church assumes a responsibility for the totality of man — his body and his spirit. All over the world, the church, the "Ins," the sheep, attempt to supply man with bread. And we claim to have more than bread for the body, which really is not difficult to supply. We offer the bread of life. The Shepherd of the "Ins" reminds the world that "Man shall not live by bread alone." And he boasts of being the "bread of life." "I was hungry and you gave me to eat."

Voice of the Outs: But not bread, man! Not bread! Not gold! Not dust! Not dough! Not that unleavened bread on which your society is run! Oh no. That's the bread that makes the world go round. Money! I have watched you for a hundred, for a thousand years. And out of all your articulations, out of all your speeches, I have extracted that one thing, and I know it. Yes, man does live by bread — money — cash! "Take the cash," says the poet, "and let the credit go." Credit, you know, is something for us goats. It comes too high, and we pay too dear, because we don't know any

better. We're out — way out. We know that
bread is what makes people go. And it
makes you go. Where, we think you don't
know. But we will follow you.

Voice of the Ins: "I was thirsty, and you gave me drink." Man
has nothing in him but thirst. From his first
day to his last he is athirst. He marries because he is thirsty for love. He works because he thirsts for what his labor can buy.
He educates himself because he thirsts for
knowledge and meaning for his life. Man
acts to satisfy his insatiable thirst. And those
in the white skins say that man cannot find
his satisfaction in his knowledge, or in his
labor, or in what he earns, or in what he
loves. Though these be good, they do not
ultimately quench man's thirst. And the
reason is that man has a deeper thirst — a
thirst for God. And the Lord of the sheep
says, "Happy are those who hunger and
thirst after righteousness." And he adds,
"The water that I shall give him will become in him a spring of water welling up
into eternal life." "Lord," the sheep ask,
"When did we see you?" "I was thirsty and
you gave me drink."

Voice of the Outs: Strong drink. To keep me from remembering
where I was. Out there in the desert. Down
there in the inner city. Chained. Fettered.
Shackled. Everything taken from me. Myself
deprived of freedom. You gave me drink —
strong drink — so I could forget I was not
free. That I bore upon my back the whole
burden of your sins. And you put me where
I am. Now, as I follow you into your great
cities, and follow your messages, you send
me drink. Polluted water from your suburban cesspools. And you expect me to be
grateful and to thank you for driving me
into the desert where no man can drink.

Voice of the Ins: "I was a stranger and you welcomed me." Where are the strangers in our midst? You say there are none in this day of population explosion? Look again, and maybe you will see Christ. For there are many lonely people in the midst of our teeming masses. David Riesman's title says it: *The Lonely Crowd.* Society is very skilled at insulating itself from certain groups. Many who are part of us dwell in isolation from us. Our strangers are to be found among the elderly. We idolize youth and let others pass away. Our strangers are forgotten children. Victims of divorce and tangled lives of parents. Born but not wanted. They are products of the irresponsible. Our strangers are the dispossessed, the disinherited. They are legion. The sheep do not have to suffer the pangs of loneliness, for they know that they are all members of the family of God. And our shepherd is in the midst of strangers and he says, "Lo, I am with you always." Surely those on the outside could say, if they would, "I was a stranger, and you welcomed me."

Voice of the Outs: Took me in, would be more like it! You sure took me all right! You fooled me with your messages about the family of God and that we are all brothers whatever the color of the skin, whatever the belief, whatever the position. You took me in, all right. You told me that if I worked hard, if I struggled upward, that I could get up. That I could stand on my own two legs, be somebody. That I could live where I could afford to live. Oh, you took me in all right, but you will not take me in. I remain undigestible. Now I've got the bread. I've got the bread, man, and I'll eat it. Bitter bread, perhaps. But you will have to accept me as I am. And that is as you have made me. You have pushed me away from God. Out into the desert, bearing, let me remind you, the burden of your transgressions. Oh, welcome me back. Let us be one. I am afraid.

Voice of the Ins: "I was naked, and you clothed me." The worst kind of nakedness is to be stripped of dignity. When dignity is lost, our humanity is lost. The world knows a great deal about nakedness. Many are cold and in misery because they are not properly clothed. The "Ins" are called to this ministry of clothing. Christ also calls his sheep to clothe all men with respect. He guides our eyes to the needy as a reminder that we can never regard them as anything less than children of God. They should never be merely statistics. They should never be merely the objects of a poverty program supported by the affluent "Ins." The Lord of the "Ins" did not say "Happy are the poor," but "Happy are the poor in spirit, for theirs is the kingdom of Heaven." The church of the in-group is called to shoulder the ministry of bringing respect to every man. It is the voice of Christ that calls, and we must answer. "Lord, when did we see you?" "I was naked, and you clothed me."

Voice of the Outs: With what? Your outworn rags? Or even if they were good, did you give them that I might wear them in abject gratitude? Did you give them to me so that you might be glad you could give? Did you simply need me to remind you how well off you are? How important I am, because I am not you. A clothes horse, perhaps. Someplace to put yesterday's fashion. Think. The burden of your transgression, your guilt, my desert.

Voice of the Ins: "I was sick, and you visited me." Sickness stalks the earth. It marks the faces of men and scars the very earth on which we live.

Sickness touches more than the bodies and spirits of people. It reaches into the world itself and tears it into pieces — into East and West, into North and South. Life is broken. Who can make it whole? Who will bring healing? When the sheep of the parable ministered to the sick, it is not stated that they healed them, only that they visited them. The essence of health is harmony. And when the white sheep look out over the world, they see not only its brokenness, but also him who makes us whole. We see not only sickness, but also the great physician who shows a vision of a new heaven and a new earth. But He will not let the sheep stand by and dream dreams. He who knows the healer must heal. He who would be near the physician must go among the sick. "Lord, when did we see you?" "I was sick, and you visited me."

Voice of the Outs: Where? How could you get there? The hospital I go to is two hours by bus from the place where I live. How did you find me? Were you there when they crucified my child? When they told me that I needed to wait in line? That I wasn't really an emergency? Were you there? I don't remember you there. I was there. I watched my child, I held my child, I cradled my child in my arms, and I loved my child, and my child died and I waited. Were you there? Did you visit me? Could you find me? That massive hospital in the middle of the desert where I live — downtown. Were you there? I was.

Voice of the Ins: "I was in prison, and you came to me." There are many ways to be imprisoned. Men can be held behind steel bars, or behind walls, as in Berlin. They can also be in bondage to the ideas and values which hold them. The ideology of communism imprisons as much as does a wall. So does prejudice. Most of the world is not really free. Most of the world is in prison. Because he cuts himself off from other people, the biased man confines the world in which he lives, and builds his own prison. The sheep say that there is only one way to freedom. It comes through commitment to Jesus Christ. He said, "You shall know the truth and the truth shall make you free." Yes, freed from hatred and free to love. Freed from death, and free to live. Freed from fear, free to act. "I was in prison and you came to me."

Voice of the Outs: Yeah, you came. But why? To congratulate yourselves that it was I, not you, who was there? To see that I had gotten my just deserts? That I was being properly punished for my terrible sin, my iniquitous crimes? Why did you come? Did you come to comfort me? Did you come to free me? Did you come to see me, or to see what you might have been, had our places been reversed? I am in prison, and it is you who jailed me.

I am hungry. I am thirsty. I seem strange to you because I am not with you, nor above you. You see my nakedness and are ashamed for me. You see me sick, and do not minister unto me. You see me in prison, because of my lack of teaching, of education, and most especially of love. So, though you will pray *for* me, it is not often you pray *with* me. I ask you now, let us pray.

Voice of the Ins: O Lord of all sheep and all goats, we do not ask for wisdom to be able to tell the difference, but only for the power to be sheep. Amen.

DIALOGUE OF CONFLICT: "DON'T BLAME GOD"

THIS IS A RATHER DRAMATIC TRIALOGUE sermon in which two worshipers react to an unseen "devil's advocate" who startles everyone by breaking into a reading of the Twenty-third Psalm. His part was pre-recorded, complete with echo effect, and the mysterious voice was piped through two stereo speakers placed under the front pews on either side of the sanctuary. The two worshipers were seated in the congregation and seemed to "think out loud." As they voice their reflections, the difference between their two viewpoints becomes obvious, and the rest of the congregation is forced to consider its own hypocrisy and re-examine its own convictions.

Apparently this sermon was carefully and thoroughly prepared. Pastor Howard E. Friend writes:

> The writing of the sermon grew out of a discussion group that I conduct as Auxiliary Chaplain of the small Air Force installation nearby the church. We had gotten one evening into a rather intense discussion on the philosophical problem of evil and the practical question of human need. This then occupied our conversation for several weeks. Somehow, I'm not really sure just how, the idea was conceived of presenting our thoughts to the congregation in the form of some dialogue. The "devil's advocate" format was suggested by one of the boys. It took us several weeks, both to develop the structure and write the text. Each participant with assistance from friends pretty much wrote his own section.

The date of the sermon was March 5, 1967, which the church had designated as the "One Great Hour of Sharing" Sunday, and the sermon was aimed at that theme. Perhaps it is the first example of an effective sermon ever written by a committee! The congregational response was good, the pastor writes, even though many people were startled by the unexpected interruption. On this occasion some real listening apparently took place.

"DON'T BLAME GOD"

Written and presented by the Rev. Howard E. Friend, Jr., with Robert Shortino, Ron Van Norstrand, Ron Fountain, Andy Borgogna, and Richard Swartout of the Montauk, New York, Air Force Station

Minister:	Hear the word of God as it is written in the Twenty-third Psalm: "The Lord is my shepherd, I shall not want."
	Think about that.
Devil's Advocate:	Yes, do think about that. Oh, maybe I'd better repeat it for those who were sleeping instead of really listening: "The Lord is my shepherd, I shall not want." Hmmpf. Congratulations, Reverend Friend. You're doing another wonderful job of lulling the people into complacency. You stroll over from your comfortable split level and talk to your comfortable people all these comfortable words. Well, this time I'm not going to let you get away with it.
	By the way, folks, don't look for me. You can't find me or see me. But I can find you — any of you — whenever I desire. Who am I? Oh, let's just say a voice. Conscience? No, not that voice — the other one.
	Now you know, Reverend, you *are* right — all of you are right. The Lord *is your* shepherd, you shall not want. But I could take you on a little tour; no place farther than a few hours by jet from where you're sitting — and show you some other people.
	— I'd show you a little boy in Korea, playing alone; yes, always alone. You see, he's got leprosy. His skin is brown and

ugly; and it's peeling off his body. Is the Lord his shepherd?

— I'd show you a farmer in India. Ha, that's a laugh; a farmer in India. Too poor to buy seed; dry, dusty soil; the third year of drought. Is the Lord his shepherd?

— I'd show you a little boy in Pakistan who's so skinny that his ribs stick out. He'd find a banquet in your garbage can. Is the Lord his shepherd?

"Just isolated cases," you're thinking? Maybe . . . but maybe not! Do you know that a third of the world goes to bed hungry at night? Do you know that you spend more on garbage removal than the average family in India spends on food? Do you know that most of the dogs in your prosperous country get better medical care than half the people of the world?

What are you reading about, there, Reverend? A part-time shepherd? Or only for the right kind of sheep? Doesn't his territory include India or Pakistan or Hong Kong? "The Lord is my shepherd, I shall not want." Hah!

First Worshiper: You know, as much as I hate to admit it, there's some truth in what he (whoever he is) says. And gosh, it's not just over there in Asia or Africa or out there in Los Angeles, either. I just rode through that awful part of Springs last week. Those one-room shacks for families of four and five. Coal stoves that keep it just above freezing on cold nights. I bet they don't have much to eat at night, either. . . . Or what about those Long Island Indians: the Shinnecocks in Southampton and the Poosepatucks in Mastics. Maybe Indians are a minority we've forgotten about today. . . . I guess there are some people right near by who could find this psalm hard to say and feel.

Maybe the Lord didn't plan far enough ahead when he made this earth! Maybe he didn't count on so many poor people being born; maybe he didn't know there wouldn't be enough food and all to go around. Maybe this psalm was O.K. a long time ago, but it doesn't seem to be very true today.

But wait a minute: that's not right. I know it can't really be the Lord's fault. Of course, it's not God's fault — it's the poor people's fault! Let's face it. We all know how lazy those lower-class people are. And we know that the Bible says, "God helps those who help themselves." (Or, at least, I *think* the Bible says that.) But anyway, if they're too darn lazy to work, it sure isn't my fault they haven't got enough to eat.

Besides, look at us. We're all hard working people and none of us are starving. If they'd spend less time complaining how bad off they are and get to work, then I know for a fact they wouldn't starve. Sure, there are a lot of poor and needy people in the world. But it's not God's fault; and it's not my fault either. It's their own fault.

"The Lord is my shepherd, I shall not want"— of course, because I've worked hard and I deserve it!

Second Worshiper: Boy, the devil, or whoever he is, sure talks a good line. There *are* lots of folks who might find that psalm hard to say. But it certainly isn't God's fault. You know, it's not that he hasn't given us enough to go around; it's what we've done with it. We waste it, hoard it, misuse it. We don't distribute it or share it. Why, God gave us clean, flowing rivers — we dumped the industrial waste into them. He gave us clean, pure air — we pumped it full of exhaust and fumes. He gave us great, thick forests — we cut them down without replanting; the floods are really our fault. And then here we sit, filling our storage bins to overflowing with grain, and then building more; all the while India is starving. No, it's not God's fault; he *is* a good shepherd. But then, whose fault is it?

Maybe it is the poor man's fault himself. But somehow that just doesn't ring true. If a guy can't get a job or can't get ahead because his skin is black, that's surely not his fault. And if we've stopped using coal for fuel and all a guy knows is mining, it can't be all his fault. And those poor, hungry babies in India, they didn't have any choice where they were being born.

You know, it's not a matter of their being lazy and my working hard; it's just that I've been darn lucky, and I can hardly take any credit for luck, much less blame someone else for bad luck. The chances were fifteen to one against my being born an American; and here we sit with two-fifths of the world's money. I was just lucky, that's all.

But you know, I can share my good luck. That little boy in Korea could be cured of leprosy if there was a hospital nearby. If that farmer had tools and seed and fertilizer and if he knew how to irrigate, he could till that soil. And certainly we all have enough food to share some with that skinny boy in Pakistan. No, I can't pack up and go there myself; none of us can. But that "One Great Hour of Sharing." It *can* go there, if we give it the support.

"The Lord is my shepherd, I shall not want." Maybe that means lots of things. It could be a promise (something that can be true) ; or a prayer (something that we want to be true, with God's help) ; or a challenge (because we've prevented it from being true); or a commitment (something we can help become true for all people). . . .

Minister: ". . . He makes me to lie down in green pastures. He leads me beside still waters; he restores my soul."

Devil's Advocate: Ah, folks, isn't that just beautiful? Green pastures . . . still waters . . . a restored soul. Look up at that stained-glass window in front. (You know, the one you look at every week during the sermon, when Reverend Friend thinks you're looking at him.) That window is the world, isn't it? At least, *your* world! Peaceful, serene, calm — real green pastures. I really envy you people who live here.

You don't have to worry about a C-47 plane equipped with defoliation spray coming over that hill, do you? Do you know what it would look like when that airplane had passed? A mound of barren dirt! How many green pastures are left in Vietnam? . . . Yes, listen to those soothing words the reverend is reading and think of your rolling hills and your little world at the end of Long Island. "He leads me beside still waters; he maketh me to lie down in green pastures." But not in Central Park after dark!

But wait a minute. That's all very far away, isn't it? That just has nothing to do with Montauk. I can't expect you folks to worry about someone else's problems. Your "paths of righteousness" are right here. You live by the Ten Commandments. You come to church. If I were you, I'd just enjoy those green pastures and still waters — and not ask a lot of questions.

First Worshiper: Here we go again! But you know something, devil, you're off base on this one. You only talk about the evil and destruction (although I kinda guess that's all closer to your line of work); but I just don't think things are all that bad. I think we do lots of good things that we deserve credit for.

How about civil rights? Congress has made it a law that the Negroes in this country will have the same rights as the rest of us. And people in Montauk are certainly doing their share to advance civil rights; you'll never see any discrimination here. Why, some of my best friends are Negroes. And, after all, there are bad in all races. As long as they keep their place, I'm all for integration.

And just look at all the charity we give to the poor people. Why, we give more than any other people on the earth. If it wasn't for our generosity, millions more would starve.

Of course there's evil in the world; but that's really just a few ripples on the still waters. And we've done just all that we can about them. I'm sure I can't be expected to get too worried about it all. You can't expect me to lose sleep over everybody else's problems. That's one of the reasons I came to Montauk — just to get

evil" — great words, but I don't think your God can pull it off!

First Worshiper: Ouch! That one really touches a sore spot. Oh, I guess if it was just an intellectual question I could handle it. But it's when questions like that come out of experience that it really hurts. Of course I believe that the Lord is always with us. But what do I say to the man who has looked forward for years to retirement, and then finds out that he has cancer? What do I say to the mother of a little child crushed by a speeding truck? How do I fathom why some men prosper and live long lives, while others suffer or are snuffed out in the prime of life?

Central Islip, like all of the mental hospitals, filled to capacity as more and more people suffer mental breakdowns. Divorce rates up sharply; also suicides, crime rates, narcotics.

That psalm sure was right on one count — we do walk through the valleys!

Second Worshiper: But maybe, just maybe, that's the point. That we can walk *through* the valley. Not "Even though I walk within the valley," not "even though I walk only in the valley," but "even though I walk *through* the valley." And maybe there's no other way to go; maybe there's no mountain without a valley as well.

After all, what do we remember most about Jesus? Sure, he changed the water to wine to keep that wedding party going. And he fed the thousands of people; he healed the blind and lame; he told the disciples where to catch fish. But for all the things he said, we remember him more for one thing he did. He suffered and died. Funny, isn't it. We really wish it weren't so. But: no cross, no resurrection; no Good Friday, no Easter morning; no defeat, no victory. Without that deepest of valleys, there is not that highest of mountains. God didn't talk us out of the valley. He didn't try to tell us "it really isn't that bad." He came down there with us, and led us out.

But you know, that's true of people too. Sometimes you only feel really close to someone when they're suffering and you suffer with them. Like when Frank's father died; that's when we really became close friends. You really find yourself when you find someone else who needs you.

And, you know: that Korean kid with leprosy, and that Indian farmer, and the poor folks in Springs, and all the rest, they need more than my money. They need me and I need them. Of course, that's what charity really is: loving and sharing with your neighbor.

COMPOSITE DIALOGUE: "YOU ARE THE MAN"

THIS SERMON BEGINS as an enlargement of the biblical dialogue between David and Nathan; then there is a break in the action, and the two persons step out of their biblical roles to make contemporary comments about the Christian's attitude toward sex. Thus the sermon moves from a conflict situation into a more supportive relationship between the participants, and it closes with a prayer that blends biblical and contemporary language in its voicing of the guilt, contrition, and hope of modern man in the sight of his God. The hope expressed is "Create in me a clean heart, O God, and put a new and right spirit within me."

"You Are the Man" was presented at the First Baptist Church of Fredericktown, Ohio, to a congregation of middle-class, non-professional people. The one prop used was a crown worn by David during the biblical scene to identify him immediately as king, but other devices might be used to lend dramatic effect, such as a brown tunic worn by the prophet. The biblical scene might center upon a chair in the middle of the chancel which would represent David's throne; when the biblical scene was over, the participants would drop their props and move from the center to the pulpit and lectern on either side. The ensuing discussion would take the form of a commentary upon ideas suggested by the David-Nathan dialogue as those ideas relate to the current morality and behavior. Such a dialogue sermon may not only enlighten people by presenting a Christian concept of sex — it may also force persons to recognize their own guilt, assess their own attitudes and behavior, and rededicate themselves to an ideal they had previously rejected or ignored. Hopefully a certain catharsis may take place within those who become involved in the dialogue while it is taking place.

"YOU ARE THE MAN"

Gordon C. Bennett

David: (REFLECTIVE) This being king is so lonely, so lonely. It is a grand, glorious life, but such a lonely life. Its conquests feed the ego but its solitude is chastening. But I should shake off melancholy. Right now we're on top of the world! We are dealing harshly with the Ammonites and their stumbling allies, the Syrians. I have myself slain a horde of those silly Syrians with their silly armor. We have utterly routed the enemy and put them to flight! I have returned the victor to Jerusalem, heralded and praised by all the lusty voices of a joyful city. I have been feted and admired; women have thrown themselves at my feet; the most skillful musicians have tuned their harps, and the bards and minstrels of a hundred tribes have come to turn my heart with their music.

And so the shadow of gluttonous pride haunts my footsteps and swells my head. It is so difficult to rule wisely when one is successful. It is hard to swallow the hero role and give up the glory of battle for the details and duties of administrator and judge. But I am home on vacation now. I have sent Joab, my right arm, and with my finest troops he is wringing the necks of the Ammonites, and soon they will not dare to spit in the face of Israel.

It is a grand life, but a lonely one, having to be king. Whom can I talk to? I have no one with whom I can share the deepest burdens of my soul; there is no one to whom I can pour out the cares of the nation which I carry. The king is protected from all people, he is insulated from the people, he bears their sorrows alone. That is why they crown him king, that he might be torn by the responsibilities they will not bear themselves. But am I all-knowing, all-powerful, all-enduring? No. I am mortal. I am a lonely man who wrestles nightly with the problems of a nation, and who needs someone to whom he may reveal and unfold the deepest secrets of his heart. It is natural that I should seek and find such a person. She is my love, for she understands. It is lonely to be a king, so dreadfully lonely. . . . But she understands.

Nathan: (DRAWN-OUT CALL, AS COMING FROM A DISTANCE) David! David!

David: She is the apple of my eye, the bright and shining star. She is the jewel in the crown of life that out-shines all the other gems. Without her I cannot succeed, with her I cannot fail. She understands the burden I must carry, she knows the terrible agony of royalty. . . . It is so lonely to be a king.

Nathan: (AS BEFORE) David!

David: She is so lovely that surely God has made her for myself. He has created beauty in women, but in her all other beauty is dwarfed and made ugly. She is my love, my other half, the mother of my son. She un-

	derstands. We know each other. . . . It is so lonely to be a king.
Nathan:	(CLOSE, INSISTENT) David!
David:	What? Who calls? Is someone calling King David?
Nathan:	Yes. It is I, Nathan.
David:	The prophet?
Nathan:	None other in the King's court calls himself Nathan.
David:	So it is you. The prophet Nathan, the man of God. I trust you are not going to disturb me tonight with some dire prediction. I am tired.
Nathan:	I must say what must be said. I come with a message from God Almighty.
David:	Proceed, prophet. No one is denied a hearing at the court of David — not even God.
Nathan:	Listen, King. Once there was a rich man who had many flocks and herds; and a poor man who had but one little lamb which he had bought. One day a visitor came to the home of the rich man, but instead of killing the animals in his own fields to prepare a table for his guest, the rich man took the lamb that belonged to the poor man, the only lamb he owned, and he killed it and prepared it for the traveler who had come to his house. What say you, King David?
David:	Cursed be the man who has done this! That rich man deserves to die! I shall have his head torn from his body, for he has not shown mercy and kindness to his poor neighbor. But first I shall make him give the poor man four lambs to atone for the one he has taken. What man in Israel would do such a thing? I will strangle him with my bare hands! Where is this man that I may have him arrested! Who is the person you're talking about? Where is he? Who is he?
Nathan:	(PAUSE. THEN DELIBERATELY) You are the man.
David:	(DUMBFOUNDED) What? Is this some fool joke, Nathan?
Nathan:	It is no joke. Thus says the Lord, the God of Israel: I anointed you King over Israel, and I delivered you out of the hands of Saul; and I gave you your master's house, and your master's wives, and I gave you the house of Israel and of Judah; and if this were too

little, I would add to you so much more. Why have you despised the word of the Lord, to do what is evil in his sight? You have smitten Uriah the Hittite with the sword, and you have taken his wife to be your wife, and you have slain Uriah with the sword of the Ammonites. Now therefore, says the Lord, I will raise up evil against you and your house; and because by this deed you have utterly scorned the Lord, the child that is born to you shall surely die. Thus says the Lord.

David: I can't believe it.

Nathan: You had better believe it.

David: I can't believe it. God has anointed me King. He has entrusted me with this nation. Will he turn against me in a moment?

Nathan: Are you exempt from his demands? Does your royal robe give immunity? Are you not subject to the moral conditions of the covenant? Does not the Seventh Commandment apply also to you, King David?

David: "Thou shalt not commit adultery." But I am King! God has given me wives and concubines for my pleasure. Surely Bathsheba is mine by virtue of. . . .

Nathan: The divine right of kings? What about the divine right of the people, the right to freedom from search and seizure, the right of every man to the pursuit of wedlock without having to stave off the designs of another? What about the right of every man to happiness without having to fear the king's assassins after dark? What about the rights of your subjects, King David?

David: Well — I — I am not to blame for this, Nathan. It was the woman who enticed me. After all, she didn't have to stand by that open window! It was Bathsheba — she deliberately lured me to her abode! What if you happened to see a woman bathing, Nathan, and that woman was oooooh! Surely the spark of maleness would rise and engulf you, Nathan, even you. Love is powerful, Nathan, the urge within you to love and be loved. It is a smoldering flame ready at any moment to break into a raging fire that consumes everything within reach. Given the right incentive, given the catalyst, given the thrill of the moment!

Nathan: And have you no power of will, David? Are you captive to your inner passion, enslaved by it completely? This love you felt, was it love or lust? You were not attracted by her personality nor by her character, the cutting edge of her mind or the purity of her spirit. You were lured by the beauty of her body!

David: But is this not part of God's plan? He made man and woman, and he made them attractive to each other. Am I to shun the obvious charms of —

Nathan: You speak as if man was an animal who could do nothing except respond to the stimuli around him. If that were so, there would be no guilt in this. But you are a man, David, one jump above the animals. You have knowledge of good and evil, the freedom to choose the higher way, the opportunity to respond to the challenge of God. And yet you are not just a man — you are a king who is to set the example for other men. Where is your will, David? A woman bathing herself. What if she did it deliberately? Are you an animal, that you cannot say no to the fire within? Is the King but a camel or a panther? Is no man's wife safe from King David?

David: Nathan, don't push me too far. Even prophets may lose their heads.

Nathan: You cannot scare me.

David: Look here: chief among God's creations is the gift of sex. From the beginning he has made male and female to enjoy each other's company. Love is a gift to be enjoyed, otherwise he would not have given it to us. If I see a ripe olive, I pick it.

Nathan: And if the olive tree belongs to another's orchard?

David: Then —

Nathan: And what if you compound your guilt by having that man killed?

David: Now wait —

Nathan: By having him put in the forefront of battle so that he would be sure to fall?

David: What? Lies! Who told you this?

Nathan: Enough! You cannot fence with me.

David: I'm not responsible! Joab had him put at the head of the charge! Uriah was a skilled warrior. Naturally, Joab wanted him up front to lead the company. Don't lay his death to my account. A hundred men die in battle every day. The Hittite was just one of the casualties of the war.

Nathan: Is God blind that you can fool him? He knows!

David: So he knows. All right. Nathan, I didn't want to issue that order but he forced my hand. That fool would not — he just, just would not act like a normal soldier on furlough. It was his own fault I had to kill him! The stupid Hittite would not go home to Bathsheba that night. I urged him, I begged him, I pleaded with him, but to no avail. Some sense of loyalty he had! "I won't go home to my wife," he said, "why should I dwell in comfort when Joab and my colleagues are camping out in the open field?" That clod! He gave me no out! There was no way to make it seem like his child! It was his own fault! Why didn't he go home to his wife? He must not have loved her; everyone knows they were unhappy together.

Nathan: Does that make it right?

David: No. No, it was wrong! (BREAKING INTO REMORSE) It was wrong! It was my shame, my sin to commit murder in the name of love. It is surprising, Nathan, how easily one guilty act leads to a more dreadful thing. (WITH BITTERNESS) Aaagh! You holy man, what do you know about these things? You, the high and mighty, the secluded, the righteous one (HEAVY SARCASM HERE), what do you know about the deep needs and fierce desires of men? Bathsheba was lonely, I was lonely, and it seemed we were meant for each other's arms. Don't you understand my stark loneliness?

Nathan: I know that you are King.

David: Then you know how lonely it is to be King.

Nathan: I speak only the word of God, David! You are the man!

AT THIS POINT THERE IS A PAUSE, AND WE MOVE FROM THE BIBLICAL
SCENE TO A MODERN COMMENTARY. IF THE CHARACTERS HAD SUG-
GESTIVE COSTUMES, THEY NOW REMOVE THEM AND CONVERSE FROM
PULPIT AND LECTERN IN THEIR SUITS AND TIES.

David: Well _____, that's a dramatic scene from the
              Old Testament. What do you think of the lattice-
              work of excuse that David carved to rationalize his
              deed?

Nathan: Well, that was pure speculation by the author of this
              dialogue, _____, but it sounded real. It sounded
              so much like the kind of rationale used today by the
              advocates of sexual freedom and the so-called new
              morality.

David: This new morality sounds more like the old immor-
              ality to me. At least the way it's expounded by
              Mickey Spillane and the writers of some stories in
              Playboy. If the new morality involves wife-switching,
              non-virgin clubs, and chain marriage, I'd say there's
              nothing moral about it.

Nathan: I'll agree that our standards of sexual conduct are
              changing. Today's society seems to be characterized by
              lack of a moral code, rather than a different kind of
              code. And the church has failed to keep pace with the
              new attitudes that developed as a reaction to the old
              Victorian prudery and Puritan legalism. Too bad,
              because now it's almost too late.

David: Are you saying that the church should revamp its
              moral stand to conform to the trend towards prom-
              iscuity and free love?

Nathan: No such thing! In the first place, I'm not certain that's
              the trend today, although I will admit there is a
              greater sexual freedom and less concern about follow-
              ing an absolute moral code. But what I am saying is
              that the church needs to develop a theology of sex
              that is relevant to the situation in which modern
              youth find themselves. The movies, TV, modern liter-
              ature, many factors have cojoined in removing the
              wraps from sex, and the church must do so too. Now
              I don't mean that the way it sounded!

David: I hope not, _____.

Nathan: I mean it's time for the church to be honest and open about this topic. Surely you agree that Christian people have been silent too long.

David: Agreed. Away with the hush-hush attitude that made the topic unmentionable. Now we're having it examined even by the pulpit. Thank God for Helmut Thielicke and others.

Nathan: We can't just ignore sex and expect it to go away. And it's wrong to treat it as if it were sticky or dirty. Sex itself is not sinful, and no amount of preaching will convince people of this when they know in their hearts "it ain't so!"

David: It is clear now that sex is essentially a good gift of God. The Bible reveals love as the highest spirit of life, and the sex act is the most physical demonstration of that love between man and woman — a fulfillment of their love, in a real sense, holy and sacred.

Nathan: And we must help young men and women to see that the fulfillment of sex is to be shared within the fulfillment of love —

David: And the framework of that love is marriage.

Nathan: For only in marriage have man and woman fully given themselves to each other, for good or bad, for richer for poorer, for ever and ever.

David: Was that in the ceremony?

Nathan: Till death do us part!

David: You read the fine print, didn't you. Seriously, _____, restricting sex relations to marriage may not be what the thrill seekers want to hear, those who treat sex as a toy and the body as a commodity to be bought and sold.

Nathan: Right. You know, the expression "to have fun" has become more and more synonymous with having sex relations. This new meaning is symbolic of our sexual degradation.

David: But we've admitted that sex is fun. Haven't we?

Nathan: No question. God meant it to give pleasure, though that is not its primary function. And within the bonds of real love it can be a great joy and the highest thrill. But it's still a sacred act of procreation, and thus it is also very serious business, and sometimes even tragic. When I think of the unwanted babies born because of young people wanting to "have fun" . . . well, my point is that if sex is only a matter of fun to Johnny Jones or Sue Smith, then it's no longer even funny. Because Johnny and Sue are using a holy act of love just as a means of getting their kicks. All they want is personal pleasure.

David: You say personal, but you mean impersonal. What's wrong with sex is when people depersonalize it, strip from it the relationship of real concern for each other, to say nothing of responsibility for each other.

Nathan: Real love, lasting love, responsible love is absent. Johnny and Sue have cheapened their bodies by a relationship without meaning.

David: But that's not the end of it. If they are normal human beings with consciences, they're going to feel guilty about it. Even in this super-sophisticated age, young people are finding it hard to throw off the moral structures of the past. They may laugh it off on the outside, but inside they're churning. Result? Anxiety, neurosis, spiritual illness.

Nathan: Which reminds me of a story I heard recently, _____. A college girl came to her chaplain all in a tizzy and she said, "Do you think I'm crazy?" He said, "Of course not. What makes you think you're crazy?" "Well," she said, "when I have sex relations I feel guilty about it afterwards. My friends say, 'you're crazy.' Am I?"

David: We need more people who are crazy enough to have consciences. I hate to think what happens to society when nobody feels guilty anymore about breaking moral codes. But the fact is that more and more Americans worship at the shrine of Eros. We worship the body beautiful. Sexual stimuli bombard us every day from the billboards, the magazines, the television screens of America. It makes it extremely difficult for young people to escape the vicious trap of Diana and the lure of Eros. We have enthroned the goddess of pleasure and in the process we have crucified the personality.

Nathan: I'd like to put it this way, _____. According to Christian standards, we are called upon to love people and use things. Instead, we tend to love things and use people. Sex is a prime example. The boy and girl in the back seat of a parked car in the passion pit are out to use each other. There is probably no abiding love in their relationship. They exploit each other and thereby make of the person a thing. The main idea is to have a night of fun, no matter what the consequence to the other person.

David: Not every kid goes to the drive-in for that reason, _____. But I get the point about those who do. Not that we can pass judgment on them. None of us are pure enough to condemn the young people who make sex into a god. All of us who are adults — physically, if not mentally — have faced the problems of sex and we know something about the pressures that youth are subjected to.

Nathan: Rather than condemning those who fall, let's make a point to commend those who remain standing despite the tensions of modern living. These kids realize that pleasure is empty when pursued for its own sake.

David: Yes, if sex is regarded as pleasure only, it often leaves the participants lonely and disappointed.

Nathan: That is what the theologian Helmut Thielicke warns us about when he says that Eros may leave no room for Agape. And he says that Agape lives not by making claims but by loving.

David: That was King David's problem. His lust for Bathsheba was like laying claim to another person.

Nathan: But at least he did have a conscience, and he finally admitted his sin. Did you know that one of the psalms is supposed to be a prayer of contrition uttered by David after his encounter with Nathan forced him to his knees?

David: You must mean Psalm 51.

Nathan: Yes. There's something for all of us. Would you read the familiar section?

David: Gladly. (READS PSALM 51:1-12 OR THROUGH VERSE 17)
Nathan: Let us pray.
            O great God of goodness, light, and beauty,
            Forgive our use of people as things;
            Forgive our worship of Diana and Eros;
            Forgive our lack of concern for another;
            Forgive our lack of respect for the person;
            Forgive our misuse of the gift called sex.
Both: Create in me a clean heart, O God,
            And renew a right spirit within me.
David: Help us to appreciate beauty without exploiting it;
            Help us to enjoy the body without degrading it;
            Help us to love without lust.
            Give us the strength to keep our physical impulses in
               check.
            Make us aware of the dignity of the person.
Both: Create in me a clean heart, O God,
            And put a new and right spirit within me.
Nathan: Purge me with hyssop and I shall be clean,
David: Wash me, and I shall be whiter than snow.
Both: Create in me a clean heart, O God,
            And put a new and right spirit within me.